I0211496

LIVING WITH GRACE

LIVING WITH GRACE

John Denver Spirituality in Song and Word:
An Abecedarian of Themes

MARK G. BOYER

RESOURCE *Publications* · Eugene, Oregon

LIVING WITH GRACE
John Denver Spirituality in Song and Word: An Abecedarian of Themes

Copyright © 2025 Mark G. Boyer. All rights reserved. Except for brief quotations in critical publications or reviews, no part of this book may be reproduced in any manner without prior written permission from the publisher. Write: Permissions, Wipf and Stock Publishers, 199 W. 8th Ave., Suite 3, Eugene, OR 97401.

Resource Publications
An Imprint of Wipf and Stock Publishers
199 W. 8th Ave., Suite 3
Eugene, OR 97401

www.wipfandstock.com

PAPERBACK ISBN: 979-8-3852-5575-7
HARDCOVER ISBN: 979-8-3852-5576-4
EBOOK ISBN: 979-8-3852-5577-1

VERSION NUMBER 081325

The Scripture quotations contained herein are from the New Revised Standard Version (NRSV), copyright © 1989 by the Division of Christian Education of the National Council of the Churches of Christ in the U.S.A., and are used by permission. All rights reserved.

Scripture quotations taken from *The Message: Catholic/Ecumenical Edition* (TM), Copyright © 1993, 1994, 1995, 1996, 2000, 2001, 2002, 2013. Used by permission of NavPress Publishing Group.

Dedicated to

Jasper Kimmons,

Friend, employee, hope for the future

... [C]hange is the fuel of spiritual development ....

—*In the Garden*, 9

... [T]he spirit ... lives eternally.

—*John Denver Anthology*, 193

Let the word of Christ dwell in you richly;
teach and admonish one another in all wisdom;
and with gratitude in your hearts
sing psalms, hymns, and spiritual songs to God.

—Col 3:16, NRSV

John **Denver**
Living With Grace
Spirituality

Contents

Abbreviations

Bibles

NASB = New American Standard Bible
NIV = New International Version
NRSV = New Revised Standard Version
TM = The Message: Catholic/Ecumenical Edition

BCE = Before the Common Era (same as BC = Before Christ)

CB (NT) = Christian Bible (New Testament)

Acts = Acts of the Apostles
Col = Letter to the Colossians
1 Cor = First Letter of Paul to the Corinthians
2 Cor = Second Letter of Paul to the Corinthians
Eph = Ephesians
Gal = Letter of Paul to the Galatians
Heb = Letter to the Hebrews
John = John's Gospel
Luke = Luke's Gospel
Mark = Mark's Gospel
Matt = Matthew's Gospel
Phil = Letter of Paul to the Philippians
Rev = Revelation
Rom = Letter of Paul to the Romans
1 Thess = First Letter of Paul to the Thessalonians

CE = Common Era (same as AD = *Anno Domini*, in the year of the Lord)

HB (OT) = Hebrew Bible (Old Testament)

2 Chr = Second Book of Chronicles
Dan = Daniel
Deut = Deuteronomy
Eccl = Ecclesiastes
Esth = Esther
Exod = Exodus
Ezra = Ezra
Gen = Genesis
Hos = Hosea
Isa = Isaiah
Jer = Jeremiah
Job = Job
Josh = Joshua
Judg = Judges
1 Kgs = First Book of Kings
2 Kgs = Second Book of Kings
Lam = Lamentations
Lev = Leviticus
Mic = Micah
Nah = Nahum
Num = Numbers
Prov = Proverbs
Ps(s) = Psalm(s)
1 Sam = First Book of Samuel
2 Sam = Second Book of Samuel
Song = Song of Songs
Zech = Zechariah

JD = John Denver

John Denver Albums

ACT = A Christmas Together
AEJD = An Evening with John Denver
AER = Aerie
AUTO = Autograph
BHA = Back Home Again
DD = Different Directions
DE = Dreamland Express

ES = Earth Songs
FA = Farewell Andromeda
FJ = Forever, John
FTSS = The Flower That Shattered the Stone
GH3 = Greatest Hits: Volume 3
HG = Higher Ground
IAT = It's About Time
IWL = I Want to Live
JD = JD (John Denver)
JDS = John Denver Sings
OW = One World
PPP = Poems, Prayers and Promises
R&R = Rhymes and Reasons
RMC = Rocky Mountain Christmas
RMH = Rocky Mountain High
SH = Seasons of the Heart
SDD = Some Days Are Diamonds
SP = Spirit
TMT = Take Me to Tomorrow
WC = The Wildlife Concert
WIND = Windsong

OT (A) = Old Testament (Apocrypha)

2 Esd = Second Book of Esdras
Sg Three = Prayer of Azariah (Song of Three Jews)
Sir = Sirach (Ecclesiasticus)
Wis = Wisdom (of Solomon)

par(s) = paragraph(s)

Punctuation Usage

/ = indicates where one line of poetic text ends and another begins
(biblical notation) = see the specific biblical verse(s) in parentheses for more
    information
– = range of verses following a colon (8:3–4)
— = range of verses from a verse in one chapter to a verse in another chapter
    (8:3—9:4)
a, b, c = designates first (a), second (b), third (c), etc. sentence in a verse of
    Scripture or a line of poetic text

John Denver

Living With Grace

Spirituality

Introduction

In 1996, I published *"Seeking Grace with Every Step": The Spirituality of John Denver* (Springfield, MO: Leavenhouse Publications). The title of the book, *"Seeking Grace with Every Step,"* is from the song "Rocky Mountain High" on the album of the same name. While the song is a ballad about a twenty-seven-year-old man getting in touch with his spirit in the mountains, it is also a song about the force which inspires one's spirit—God, who is revealed through a lifetime of experiences. The subtitle, *The Spirituality of John Denver*, attempts to identify Denver's spirituality as a lifetime of seeking grace, seeking God, with every step at every time and in every place. Through the lyrics of his music, Denver shares with the listener how he did that. Only five hundred ninety-four copies of that signed and numbered book were ever printed. Over the past thirty years, I have been asked repeatedly to reprint that volume, which I have refused to do.

Instead of reprinting the previous book, I decided to rewrite and publish a new book on John Denver's spirituality in 2017: *Talk to God and Listen to the Casual Reply: Experiencing the Spirituality of John Denver* (Eugene, OR: Wipf & Stock). The title of that book also came from the song "Rocky Mountain High" and is also part of a line from it on Denver's 1972 album hit, *Rocky Mountain High*. That title more aptly captured the spirit that animated John Denver for fifty-three years.

The year 2027 marks the thirtieth anniversary of Denver's death. To commemorate Denver's spirituality, this book, titled *Living with Grace* from "Spirit" on the *Windsong* album, is subtitled *John Denver Spirituality in Song and Word: An Abecedarian of Themes*. More about the title and subtitle follows below.

As stated in the two previous books, I do not consider Denver religious in the usual sense of the term, such as being devoted to a particular set of beliefs or belonging to a particular ecclesial denomination. However, anyone who could sing about living with grace and talking to God and listening to the casual reply was certainly a spiritual person. Anyone who sang about grace and God had some spiritual dimension to his life. This new book guides the reader through themes found in Denver's spirituality which echo biblical themes. Because Denver's spirituality is a way of life and biblical spirituality is a way of life, the reader enters Denver's spirituality and biblical spirituality to reflect on ways he or she may live both together.

This work considers both the lyrics written by Denver alone, those written in collaboration with others, and those written by others but sang by Denver. Because the music of a song is married to the lyrics, the reader cannot hear the supporting music in this written text; thus, some important aspects of a song—such as tone, mood, and setting—are lost. I recommend listening to the John Denver repertoire on vinyl record, CD, or online.

Mark G. Boyer
2027, Thirtieth Anniversary of John Denver's Death

John Denver
Living With Grace
Spirituality

TITLE

Living with Grace

Living with Grace is taken from Denver's "Spirit" on the *Windsong* album. Basically, grace is the act of God sharing him- or herself with people. In "I Want to Live" on the *Greatest Hits: Volume 3* album, Denver repeats the I-want-to-live chorus over and over. The chorus of the song reflects Denver's spirituality: living, growing, seeing, knowing, sharing, giving, and being. Thus, living with grace means that Denver accepted the divine gift of life and lived it through growth, sight, knowledge, sharing, giving, and being himself.

John Denver

He was born Henry John Deutschendorf, Jr., on December 31, 1943, in Roswell, New Mexico. The public knew him better as John Denver. He was a trained architect, international performer, a man who wrote and sang songs about his experiences of living, and, in doing so, revealed his spirituality. This book is about the repeated spiritual themes that are found in his songs.

Denver began his career as a folk artist with The Mitchell Trio with whom he released four albums from 1965 to 1974. These albums helped to establish his music career. Performing primarily with an acoustic guitar, RCA Records released Denver's album *Rhymes and Reasons* in 1969; this led to his success as a solo artist. In 1970 two more albums were released by RCA Records: *Take Me to Tomorrow* and *Whose Garden Was This*. The success of those two albums led to two more in 1971: *Poems, Prayers and Promises* and *Aerie*.

From 1969 to 1997, Denver released twenty-three recorded albums in addition to four live albums, three Christmas albums, eight compilation albums, two collaborative albums, and multiple singles which, ultimately, made it onto a record. The music styles consist of ballads, country/western, jazz, rock, bluegrass, and love songs. Much of his music is neo-romantic, an attempt to capture in poetry and music the sights, sounds, tastes, touches, and smells of a lifetime of experiences. Of the approximately 300 songs associated with Denver, he wrote about 200 of them!

His music was popular not only for the common citizen, but also for state legislatures. The Colorado legislature adopted "Rocky Mountain High" as one of its two state songs in 2007, and the West Virginia legislature adopted "Take Me Home, Country Roads" as its state song in 2014. In 2023, Denver's "Take Me Home, Country Roads," on the *Poems, Prayers and Promises* album, was added to the Library of Congress' National Registry of Music.

Denver was one of those people who was into almost everything! He appeared in several films, and he was featured in television specials. He sang about his love of nature and worked on environmental issues, space exploration, and other issues of the 1970s through the 1990s. As noted in the lyrics of some of his songs, Denver was an introvert, who often felt misplaced and unloved and did not know where he truly belonged or whom he truly loved.

Denver reached his peak in the 1970s. In the late 1970s he had a string of four number-one songs and three number-one albums. Wearing long blond hair, wire-rimmed granny glasses, and shirts with all types of designs on them, he toured the world playing and singing songs about his experiences of living.

On October 12, 1997, at the age of fifty-three, Denver died in Monterey Bay, California, in a solo airplane crash. While piloting a two-seat, light plane, its engine failed, and he plunged into the ocean. After funeral services, his remains were cremated and his ashes scattered in the Rocky Mountains. After all that, two more albums of his music were released along with six live albums, one Christmas album, and a dozen compilation albums. Songs that had never been recorded, songs written for special events, and other songs were published in collections after his death. All of them demonstrate the appeal of this great performer, who maintains a large following even thirty years after he died.

In 1976, he and Thomas Crum founded The Windstar Foundation, housed on a 1000-acre site near Aspen, Colorado. The goal of The Windstar Foundation was to create opportunities for people of all ages, from all walks of life, to acquire the awareness, knowledge, skills, experiences, and commitment to support a healthy and sustainable future—and to demonstrate that commitment through responsible action. The foundation emphasized service through research, communication, and education through its various programs, such as EarthPulse, Aspen Global Change Institute, The Windstar Biodome Project, Choices for the Future Symposia, The Windstar Award, Connection Groups, *World Watch* magazine, and International Work/Study Programs. Also, in 1992, John Denver founded PLANT-IT 2000, a foundation which focused on planting indigenous trees on public lands in the United States and in other locations around the world.

Located in Snowmass, Colorado, Windstar was a research and education center devoted to developing workable models for scientific and technological progress which retained a sense of harmony among people working together, between humankind and the physical environment, and between everyday concerns and spirituality. After Denver died, the foundation closed its doors in October 2012, sold its property in 2013, and donated the proceeds to an Aspen charity.

The fifteen-feet-tall bronze sculpture of Denver—titled "Spirit" by Sue DiCicco—which was erected on the Windstar property in 2002, was donated to the Colorado Music Hall of Fame at Red Rocks Amphitheater, Morrison, Colorado, ten miles west of Denver. It was installed there in 2015. Denver was the first inductee to the hall of fame. The statue's name, "Spirit," echoes Denver's 1976 album of the same name, his song "Spirit" on the 1975 *Windsong* album, and depicts Denver's "The Eagle and the Hawk" on the 1971 *Aerie* album.

Henry John Deutschendorf, Jr., was married to Annie Martel from 1967 to 1982. During that time, the couple adopted two children: Zachary John Denver and Anna Kate Denver. Henry John Deutschendorf, Jr., was married to Cassandra Delaney from 1988 to (separated in 1991) 1993. One child was born during that time: Jesse Belle Deutschendorf. All three children have songs written about them; the titles of the songs include their names.

Spirituality

General

The Hebrew word for breath, wind, or spirit is *rua(c)h*. It appears about four hundred times in the HB (OT) and the OT (A). Depending on the English translation, *ruah*'s first appearance in the Bible is Genesis 1:2. *The New Revised Standard Version* (NRSV) states that a wind from God swept over the face of the waters, but has a footnote indicating that the phrase could also be translated as the spirit of God swept over the waters. *The Contemporary*

English Version (CEV) states that the Spirit of God was moving over the water. Just as we are getting started, it is important to note that the NRSV does not capitalize the s of spirit, but the CEV does! The immediate implication for the reader is to note that the reference to spirit, usually understood to be the human spirit, and the reference to Spirit, usually understood to be the divine Spirit, are indicated with lower-case or capital letters. However, in Hebrew there are no capital letters! Thus, when translators from Hebrew to English capitalize or do not capitalize the s of spirit, they are interpreting the meaning of an otherwise ambiguous text. Furthermore, translators have settled on only one meaning of the word *ruah*, which is used for breath, wind, and spirit—both human and divine! As we will see, there are many ways to plumb the many meanings of *ruah* in the HB (OT) and the OT (A).

The ambiguity associated with *ruah* does not disappear in the CB (NT). The Greek word for breath, wind, or spirit is *pneuma*. It appears nearly four hundred times. Just as in Hebrew, there are no capital letters in ancient Greek. Thus, not only is the translation of the word as breath, wind, or spirit an interpretation of the text in which it appears, but when it is translated, putting a capital S or a lowercase s on it is a further interpretation of the text. For example, in the CB (NT), the first appearance of *pneuma* in the NRSV is Matthew 1:18b: "When [Jesus'] mother Mary has been engaged to Joseph, but before they lived together, she was found to be with child from the Holy Spirit." The phrase—"from the Holy Spirit"—could just as well be translated "from the holy breath," or "from the holy wind," or even "from the holy spirit." The non-capitalized phrase in Greek is a descriptive title—not a name—for God's manifestation as a spirit being or a Spirit Being. Likewise, in Mark 2:8, Jesus perceives in his spirit (*pneuma*)—where the translators chose no capital s—but in Mark 1:10, the Spirit descends upon Jesus—where the translators chose a capital S.

In general in the NRSV, translators of the HB (OT) and OT (A) do not use a capital S for *ruah* in any of its phrases, such as the spirit of the LORD. In the CB (NT), however, translators do use a capital S for *pneuma*, especially when the word *holy* describes it. In other than Scripture texts—where I follow what the biblical editors and translators have presented—I use Spirit to refer to the divine Spirit and spirit to refer to the human spirit. Because there is no way to tell how the writer of the text intended to use either *ruah* or *pneuma*—breath, wind, or spirit—I have chosen to let the ambiguity remain in order to plumb the richness of the spiritual benefits that exist in the biblical text. In other words, just as translators decide which meaning of the words to use in English, I have decided to let the words mean all that they can mean in this work. Thus, the topic can be Spirituality or spirituality.

Spirit (spirit) exists in the HB (OT) and in the OT (A) before it appears in the CB (NT). However, the doctrine of the Trinity—one God, three coequal persons of Father, Son, and Holy Spirit—does not exist in the HB (OT), the OT (A), or the CB (NT). The doctrine of the Holy Spirit begins with the Ecumenical Council of Nicaea I in 325 CE and continues to develop until the end of the Ecumenical Council of Constantinople I in 381 CE. The issue known as *filioque*—referring to the Holy Spirit proceeding from the Father and the Son—was not settled until the Council of Florence in 1439 CE. Before doctrine, there was Scripture. Thus, in this book we are exploring *ruah*—with all its meanings—in the HB (OT) and OT (A)—and *pneuma*—with all its meanings—to reach an understanding of spirituality.

Metaphorical Language

A metaphor applies a word or phrase to somebody or something that is not meant literally but to make a comparison. An example can be found in the HB (OT) book of Exodus. The LORD tells Moses that he has filled a certain man with divine Spirit (Exod 31:3). In the way that one fills a canteen with water, God fills a man with Spirit. A simile is a figure of speech that draws a comparison between two different things, especially a phrase containing the word *like* or *as*. In the CB (NT), the author of the Acts of the Apostles describes the filling of Jesus' followers with the Holy Spirit, stating, "Divided tongues, as of fire, appeared among them, and a tongue rested on each of them" (Acts 2:3, NRSV). Thus, being filled with the Spirit is like having a tongue of fire resting on a person, turning him or her into a bush that is blazing but not consumed (Exod 3:2).

Spirit cannot be captured in words; it cannot be possessed, boxed, or defined. It is without form. That is both the beauty of ambiguity—breath, wind, and spirit—and the challenge of writing about spirituality, an English word incorporating spirit into itself. Because spirit—along with breath and wind—is invisible, to begin to comprehend spirituality, we need something visible. And the ambiguous meanings of *ruah* and *pneuma* begin to serve our needs while reminding us that the invisible Spirit and spirit are manifest or made visible through matter, but they are not matter. Thus, matter reveals Spirit, and Spirit needs matter to show itself! Matter—breath and wind—reveals Spirit to spirit—and is the means for spirit to encounter Spirit.

In biblical literature there are multiple ways that spirit can experience Spirit. However, here we are limiting ourselves to two to get at the meaning of spirituality. First, there is the Johannine thesis. In John's Gospel in the CB (NT), spirituality is Spirit connecting to spirit. It is Spirit giving birth to spirit; according to John's Gospel, ". . . [W]hat is born of the Spirit is spirit" (John 3:6, NRSV). It is Spirit breathing life into spirit; "[s]urely everyone stands as a mere breath," sings the psalmist (Ps 39:5b, NRSV). Biblically, breath signifies both the breath in a living being and the larger element of wind, the earth breathing or God sighing. Spirituality is the act of Spirit blowing wind into spirit. Because "God is spirit, . . . those who worship him must worship in spirit and truth," states the Johannine Jesus (John 4:24, NRSV). According to the HB (OT) book of Proverbs, "The human spirit is the lamp of the LORD, searching every inmost part" (Prov 20:27, NRSV).

Spirit seeks to connect to spirit to become tangible, available to the senses, since it has no form. A John Denver song does not contain the holy. Instead, holiness is experienced in the encounter with its lyrics and music. In other words, breath and wind do not contain the Spirit, but spirit encounters Spirit through the experience of breath and wind; the awareness that the experience remains vital long after the encounter is over. Mutual desiring and divine indwelling is the intended impact of Spirit connecting to spirit.

The second thesis is from the genuine Pauline letters. In his First Letter to the Corinthians, Paul explains: ". . . [A]nyone united to the Lord [Jesus Christ] becomes one spirit with him" (1 Cor 6:17, NRSV). In his Second Letter to the Corinthians, he adds, ". . . [A]ll of us . . . seeing the glory of the Lord as though reflected in a mirror, are being transformed into the same image from one degree of glory to another; for this comes from the Lord, the Spirit" (2 Cor 3:18, NRSV). Those who believe that Jesus died and God raised Christ from the dead are united to Christ Jesus, forming one body and becoming one Spirit with him. As a member of the body of Christ, we see the glory of the Spirit reflected in breath and wind, and our spirits are transformed into the same image from one degree of glory to another by the Spirit. The result is "the communion of the Holy Spirit" (2 Cor 13:13, NRSV).

Spirit in the Bible is an invisible force; it is like wind, felt but not seen. Paul presents this idea in his First Letter to the Corinthians, writing that God reveals himself "to us through the Spirit; for the Spirit searches everything, even the depths of God. For what human being knows what is truly human except the human spirit that is within? So also no one comprehends what is truly God's except the Spirit of God" (1 Cor 2:10–11, NRSV). Thus, according to Paul, we have received "the Spirit that is from God, so that we may understand the gifts bestowed on us by God. And we speak . . . in words not taught by human wisdom but taught by the Spirit, interpreting spiritual things to those who are spiritual" (1 Cor 2:12–13, NRSV). In his Second Letter to the Corinthians, the apostle adds, "Now the Lord is the Spirit, and where the Spirit of the Lord is, there is freedom" (2 Cor 3:17, NRSV). The author of the Letter to the Ephesians understood his Pauline source, writing that through Christ Jesus, we now "have access in one Spirit to the Father" (Eph 2:18, NRSV). We have access to God because the Spirit connects to our spirits and establishes a pipeline through which divine life flows. That is spirituality.

Spirit is another way to speak and write about divine presence. The Spirit of God is simply God himself. Spirit is the word for the divine presence breathed into people, hovering over people, giving life to people. It is like breath or wind, but it is not either one of those. In the CB (NT) divine presence became incarnate in Jesus of Nazareth, who was named Emmanuel, which means God is with us (Matt 1:23). The divine energy or divine power of the Spirit seeks to connect to the human spirit; this act of connecting is spirituality.

The spirit radiates energies by which the body lives and functions. Living the connection of Spirit to spirit is spirituality. The human spirit is the life principle of a body to which God connects. Therefore, by referencing the quote above from John's Gospel (4:24), we can say that the God we worship is spirit; our own spirit (which is spirit embodied) is with what we worship. This, of course, is nothing other than Spirit connected to spirit: spirituality.

Spirit becomes more and more incarnate in human flesh-embodied spirit. Spirit gives life to spirit. Our nature is a unique shaping of divine Spirit energy. According to Paul in his Letter to the Romans, the Spirit who enables us to cry, "Abba!" "Father!" bears witness with our spirit that we are children of God (Rom 8:16). In other words, Spirit outpours itself into spirit; spirit is infused with Spirit. That is why spirituality is a way of living spirit connected to Spirit. Over time each of us weaves a unique story of responsiveness to the Holy Spirit's invitations. According to Paul, ". . . [W]e speak . . . in words not taught by human wisdom but taught by the Spirit, interpreting spiritual things to those who are spiritual" (1 Cor 2:13, NRSV). That is also why Paul tells the Galatians, "Live by the Spirit . . . (Gal 5:16, NRSV).

We are surrounded by Spirit. We are immersed in Spirit. All is in the Spirit! The psalmist asks the LORD, "Where can I go from your spirit? Or where can I flee from your presence?" (Ps 139:7, NRSV) The answer is, obviously, there is no place to escape Spirit. Another such question comes from the HB (OT) book of Ecclesiastes: "Who knows whether the human spirit goes upward and the spirit of animals goes downward to the earth?" (Eccl 3:21, NRSV) The answer: No one knows. ". . . [T]he spirit of the Lord has filled the world, and that which holds all things together knows what is said," writes the author of the OT (A) book of Wisdom (1:7, NRSV). There is no clear division between Spirit and spirit; Spirit is interpenetrating spirit. Just as all things are a part of God and nothing is apart from God, so are human spirits a part of Spirit and nothing is apart from Spirit.

We spirits are so immersed in Spirit that Paul can tell the Corinthians: "To one is given through the Spirit the utterance of wisdom, and to another the utterance of knowledge according to the same Spirit, to another faith by the same Spirit, to another gifts of healing by the one Spirit, to another the working of miracles, to another prophecy, to another the discernment of spirits, to another various kinds of tongues, to another the interpretation of tongues. All these are activated by one and the same Spirit, who allots to each one individually just as the Spirit chooses" (1 Cor. 12:9–11, NRSV). Once we know that the entire physical world around us, all of creation, is both the hiding place and the revelation place for Spirit, this world becomes home, safe, enchanted, offering grace to any who look deeply. God seems to have chosen to manifest the invisible in what we call the visible, so that all things visible are the revelation of God's endlessly diffusive spiritual energy. This is why the author of the Letter to the Hebrews can write that Christ offered himself without blemish to God through the eternal Spirit (Heb 9:14). The human Jesus' spirit was connected to Spirit, just like our spirits are connected to Spirit. We see no difference between Spirit and spirit, because spirit is in or connected to Spirit; all is Spirit. Our spirit is in God.

Through the lyrics of his songs, Denver reveals his spirituality, that invisible force which motivates or inspires his personal spirit and gives insight and meaning to the way he lived his life. Spirituality, for Denver, is that energy which filled the sails of his spirit and propelled him throughout his life.

Particular

With the above background concerning the meaning of the word *spirituality*, we are ready to explore John Denver's spirituality. For Denver, spirituality was his relationship with God and the process he used to deepen it. Spirituality is all about trust of God, not fear; one does not know where it leads, only that all are on a journey. Spirituality is about change, change, and more change. It is not about supernatural revelation—visions—but about recognizing the holiness of everything and everyone around, and that is exactly what Denver did in song.

Denver's spirituality is based in nature (mountains, snow, sun, etc.). He observed nature and thoughtfully interpreted his experiences of it, recording his interpretations in lyrics and music. Denver's spirituality is also based in people, especially those he loved; after interpreting his relationships, he recorded his thoughts in love songs, which point to the divine's love for all.

Denver's spirituality is not dual. All life is an expression of God, resisted by people when it challenges privilege and power. Native Americans knew that all life is connected; from their wisdom they knew that they were a part of a unified universe, a woven field of energy or spirit. Their spiritual task was to live in peaceful harmony. Experiences of life were integrated, which is, of course, the process of becoming who one is; Denver sang about the process of becoming as an expression of the divine, because it is Spirit connecting to spirit; it is the infusion of Spirit into spirit. "Those who are spiritual discern all things," writes Paul in his First Letter to the Corinthians (2:15a, NRSV). The nature and people Denver loved nourished his spirituality.

Every action he took was related to the flow, he sang in "Relatively Speaking" on the *Seasons of the Heart* album. One person helps to make another person who he or she is, because both are immersed in spirit and Spirit. Like others, there were times when Denver didn't know who he was or what serenity meant. That is why he sang that one man can dream, love, and change the world.

Denver's spirituality begins with experience. In "Season Suite: Spring" on the *Rocky Mountain High* album, he asks his listeners if they care about what is happening around them; do their senses know the seasonal changes when they come? As he does, he wants listeners to see themselves reflected in the seasons and to see the need to carry on. Seeing oneself reflected in the seasons is but one way to come to know who one is. Denver rejoices in differences; there is no one like him in the world. However, even as different as each person is from another person, all are still the same.

Denver philosophizes about his lifetime journey asking: Where does one go if one has no way to get there? Where does one go if one has never been there before? How does one know if he or she has never been there? Spirituality, which is about change, seeks experiences, which become the object of reflection and the road map for living a spiritual life. That is why Denver sang about wanting to live, to grow, to see, to know, to share, to be—because they are the means for diving deeper. Sometimes one must lose one's self in love to find one's self.

Denver believed in God, and he sang often about him. However, he did not belong to a church. His church was the rocky cathedrals of the mountains about which he sang or flew over. His experiences of travel, mountains, seasons, etc., prompted him to write lyrics and set them to music to preserve the memories of where he had been and what he had seen and the meaning of the experiences he had in his life. In "The Chosen Ones" on the

Different Directions album, he refers to this as a message in the Bible. His sight turned inside himself in "Rocky Mountain High" on the album with the same name. He opened his mind and let the light come in, as he sings in "Season Suite: Spring" on the *Rocky Mountain High* album. He kept looking for space to find out who he was; he wanted to find his spirit-self in sunshine and dreams; he wanted to let go, to surrender, because the only thing really owned is the moment at hand. His mantra was to be all he could be; he formed truth and lived according to it.

Denver's spirituality was experienced when he was in concert. Attending a Denver concert was not only a spiritual experience, but it was a worship event. During opening remarks, he usually asked attendees (participants) to refrain from singing the verses of his songs, but to join in the choruses. Stadiums, theaters, and halls were usually full of people and song—praying, worshiping, hand in hand, being touched, experiencing spiritual unity with Denver and with others—all strangers united in song. Spirit was connected to spirit, which was connected to spirit, etc.

Both nature and people enabled Denver to know himself, to find himself, to lose himself, to live, to love, and to repeat the process over and over. Because he used his musical spirituality to share with others—whose spirituality resonated with him—they explored and enhanced their spirituality with him as a guide. Spirit touched spirit and spirit touched spirit in a spiritual experience.

in Song

The lyrics that are employed in this book come from songs on John Denver albums; the songs were written by Denver and others. Also, there are songs written by Denver which were never recorded. There are songs which were used for Windstar conferences or other gatherings which never appeared on an album. There are recorded songs which never appeared on an album, and were published after Denver's death. There are songs from a rare album which Denver published privately—*John Denver Sings*—and gave to family and friends.

To avoid copyright issues with reprinting lyrics of Denver's songs, I am not able to quote them. Thus, a paraphrase or an interpretation is used in place of the original lyrics. The name of the song is mentioned in the text along with the abbreviation for the name of the album upon which it appears. Because of the many collections of Denver's music, making some songs appear on multiple albums—such as "Rocky Mountain High" on *Rocky Mountain High, The Wildlife Concert, Earth Songs, An Evening with*

John Denver, and John Denver's Greatest Hits: Volume 1—I have chosen only one album to reference the song title. For more information consult the Bibliography and Discography at the back of this book. My hope is that the reader will enjoy this thematic spiritual and biblical analysis of John Denver's music and grow in his or her spirituality.

and Word:

The word *Word* refers to the Bible and the spirituality it contains. Denver and biblical spirituality have a lot in common; both begin with experience, reflection upon it, and a record of what the experience meant. Denver wrote songs about his experiences; biblical authors told stories, recorded reflections, narrated events, or wrote psalms and poetry about their experiences. In this book, I compare chosen Denver words with biblical material (translated from Hebrew, Aramaic, and Greek into English) and reflect on the parallel spirituality.

There is a John Denver vocabulary that matches the English translation of a biblical vocabulary. In other words, there is a limited vocabulary within the Denver repertoire of words that echoes the English words in the biblical vocabulary. For example, in the First Book of Kings, the prophet Elijah is on a journey of self-discovery which is simultaneously the discovery of God's will. He has defeated the god Baal and his 450 prophets on Mount Carmel. Then, he heads to Mount Horeb (Sinai). On the way he is directed by God where he should stop for food and water. However, to know himself, which is to know the LORD, he must get to the mountain, where all spiritual experiences began for the post-exodus Hebrews (Israelites, Jews). His experiences of God on the mountain are not the traditional earthquake, thunder, lightning, smoke, fire, etc., but a tiny whispering sound within him. After spending time listening to himself, he knows what he needs to do, leaves the mountain, and proceeds to do it (1 Kgs 18:1—19:21). Denver's spirituality begins with his experiences, continues with his reflections on them, proceed to reflection in lyrics and music, and become a record of Denver's spiritual encounters.

SUBTITLE
An Abecedarian

An abecedarian can refer to someone who is learning the basics of a subject, or it can refer to a book containing the alphabet. In this case, an abecedarian is a book whose entries are in alphabetical order. The entries in this book begin with A and end with Z. While the English alphabet is composed of twenty-six letters, there are many entries beginning with the same letter for some words shared by Denver and biblical literature.

The sixty-seven entries contained herein are not exhaustive of Denver's lyrics (words). They are merely illustrative themes of the spirituality Denver shares with biblical literature.

of Themes

Each of the sixty-seven themes draws out the parallel between Denver's lyrics and biblical perspectives. Each entry is organized with (1) a one- or two-word title; (2) a JD (John Denver) section explaining how Denver uses the word to name his experience and sing about it, and what it meant to him—the uses of the word in the JD section are not exhaustive of Denver's lyrics; (3) a Scripture passage, which illustrates the biblical use of the word—how biblical authors named their experience and what it meant for people and God; (4) a Meditation/Journal exercise to guide the reader into deeper reflection and/or journaling to deepen the reader's spirituality; Denver's experiences are universal; they are shared by many which is why his songs are still poplar thirty years after his death. And (5) a Psalm Response, a few verses from a biblical psalm (song) or canticle (song) that uses the word in some way, brings the exercise in spirituality to a close.

NOTES
on John Denver's Lyrics

In "Whispering Jesse" on the *Higher Ground* album, Jesse, a male name, is identified as a female (her) in the song; the feminine form of the male Jesse is Jessie, as it is in "I'd Rather Be a Cowboy" on the *Farwell Andromeda* album. One of Denver's daughters is named Jesse Belle.

In "Child of the Universe" on the *Seasons of the Heart* album, Denver mentions a morning dove; that type of bird is a *mourning* dove, named because of the sound it makes.

Denver often begins songs with a pronoun—you, he, she—with no antecedent noun. Usually, the listener is not told who you, he, or she is.

on the Bible

Three Parts

The Bible is divided into two parts: The Hebrew Bible (Old Testament) and the Christian Bible (New Testament). The Hebrew Bible consists of thirty-nine named books accepted by Jews and Protestants as Holy Scripture. The Old Testament also contains those thirty-nine books plus seven to fifteen more named books or parts of books called the Apocrypha or the Deutero-canonical Books; the Old Testament is accepted by Catholics and several other Christian denominations as Holy Scripture. The Christian Bible, consisting of twenty-seven named books, is also called the New Testament; it is accepted by Christians as Holy Scripture. Thus, in this work:

—**Hebrew Bible (Old Testament)**, abbreviated **HB (OT)**, indicates that a book is found both in the Hebrew Bible and the Old Testament;

—**Old Testament (Apocrypha)**, abbreviated **OT (A)**, indicates that a book is found only in the Old Testament Apocrypha and not in the Hebrew Bible;

—and **Christian Bible (New Testament)**, abbreviated **CB (NT)**, indicates that a book is found only in the Christian Bible or New Testament.

In notating biblical texts, the first number refers to the chapter in the book, and the second number (following the colon) refers to the verse within the chapter. Thus, HB (OT) Isa 7:11 means that the quotation comes from Isaiah, chapter 7, verse 11. OT (A) Sir 39:30 means that the quotation comes from Sirach, chapter 39, verse 30. CB (NT) Mark 6:2 means that the quotation comes from Mark's Gospel, chapter 6, verse 2. When more than one sentence appears in a verse, the letters a, b, c, etc. indicate the sentence being referenced in the verse. Thus, HB (OT) 2 Kgs 1:6a means that the quotation comes from the Second Book of Kings, chapter 1, verse 6, sentence 1. Also, poetry, such as the Psalms and sections of Judith, Proverbs, Isaiah, and others may be noted using the letters a, b, c, etc. to indicate the lines being used. Thus, Ps 16:4a refers to the first line of verse 4 of Psalm 16; there are two more lines of verse 4: b and c.

Because there may be a difference in the verse numbers between the *New Revised Standard Version* (NRSV) and the Vulgate (the Latin translation of the Septuagint, such as *The New American Bible Revised Edition* [NABRE]), verse numbers may be off by a verse or two. This is true particularly with the Psalms, but with other books as well. Thus, NRSV Isaiah 9:2–7 is NABRE (Vulgate) Isaiah 9:1–6; NRSV Isaiah 9:2–4, 6–7 is NABRE (Vulgate) Isaiah 9:1–3, 5–6. Introductory material to Bibles usually indicates which verse-numbering is being used.

In the HB (OT) and the OT (A), the reader often sees LORD (note all capital letters). Because God's name (Yahweh or YHWH, referred to as the Tetragrammaton) is not to be pronounced, the name Adonai (meaning *Lord*) is substituted for Yahweh when a biblical text is read. When a biblical text is translated and printed, LORD (Gen 2:4) is used to alert the reader to what the text actually states: Yahweh. Furthermore, when the biblical author writes Lord Yahweh, printers present Lord GOD (note all capital letters for GOD; Gen 15:2) to avoid the printed ambiguity of LORD LORD. The Psalms in *The Message* substitute GOD (note all capital letters) for Yahweh. When the reference is to Jesus, the word printed is Lord (note capital L and lower-case letters; Luke 11:1). When writing about a lord (note all lower-case letters; Matt 18:25) with servants, no capital L is used.

In this book, *cf* (meaning *confer*) has not been used. Biblical notations placed in parentheses indicate where the reference can be found in the Bible. For example, the Second Book of Samuel records King David writing a song (2 Sam 22:1–51). The notation in parentheses is given to the reader, who may wish to look up the full reference in his or her Bible. In some instances, a few notations appear in parentheses; again, the reader may wish to see the references in their contexts.

Bibles

Most Bible readers are not aware that there is no such thing as the original Bible! The fact is: There are Bibles. First, there is the Jewish Bible, often called the Hebrew Bible; its books were collected and completed between 70 and 90 CE based on the Jerusalem canon (collection) in this order: Torah (Genesis, Exodus, Leviticus, Numbers, Deuteronomy), Prophets (Isaiah, Jeremiah, Ezekiel, etc.), and Writings (Job, Psalms, Proverbs, etc.). It is important to note the arrangement of the collected books. Second, there is—for want of a better name—the Christian Hebrew Bible, completed in the fourth century CE, but not defined until after the Reformation. It consists of Torah, Writings, and Prophets. It is important to note the (re) ordering of the collected books. Christianity took the Jewish (Hebrew) Bible and rearranged the order of its books! Then, Christianity named it the Old Testament.

The Jerusalem canon, obviously, is the collection of biblical books used in Jerusalem and its environs. A large community of Jews, however, lived in Alexandria, Egypt. To the Jerusalem canon (books in Hebrew and Aramaic) they added books in Greek, the language they spoke; this collection is the Alexandrine canon. They also translated the Jerusalem canon's books from Hebrew and Aramaic into Greek. That translation, containing books and parts of books not in the Jerusalem canon, is called the Septuagint (abbreviated LXX). Later, the Septuagint was translated into Latin; it is known as the Vulgate. Every time a book of the Bible is translated, it picks up something and it loses something; that is because there is no such thing as literary equivalence.

Thus, we have (1) the Hebrew Bible—the Jewish Bible, (2) the Hebrew Bible (Old Testament)—the rearranged books of the Hebrew Bible, and (3) the Christian Bible—twenty-seven books originally written in Greek. The Protestant Bible contains only the books in the Jerusalem canon, but rearranged into the Old Testament, plus the Christian Bible books; the Catholic Bible contains the books in the Alexandrine collection plus the Christian Bible books.

The extra books or parts of books found in the Catholic Bible (and coming from the Alexandrine collection of the Jewish Bible), but not found in a Protestant Bible, are collectively referred to as the Apocrypha or Deuterocanonical Books. They include Tobit, Judith, additions to Esther, Wisdom (of Solomon), Sirach (Ecclesiasticus), Baruch, Letter of Jeremiah, Prayer of Azariah (addition to Daniel), Susanna (addition to Daniel), Bel and the Dragon (addition to Daniel), 1 Maccabees, 2 Maccabees, 1 Esdras, Prayer of Manasseh, Psalm 151, 3 Maccabees, 2 Esdras, and 4 Maccabees. Not every Christian group, such as Catholics, accepts all the books in the Apocrypha as Scripture; for example, out of the four books of Maccabees, Catholics accept only 1 and 2 Maccabees. In Catholic Bibles, the additional books are placed with similar books. Thus, First and Second Maccabees are inserted with the historical books; the books of Wisdom and Sirach are found in the wisdom literature section.

Thus, there is no single or original Bible; there are many Bibles; it depends on what books a specific denomination or group (Jews, Christians) accepts as Scripture. The Bible that contains any book that any group accepts as Scripture is *The Access Bible* (updated edition): *New Revised Standard Version with the Apocrypha*, general editors Gail R. O'Day and David Petersen, published in New York by Oxford University Press in 1999 and updated in 2011. In 2021, the NRSV was published by Zondervan as the New Revised Standard Version updated edition (NRSVue), which, like its predecessor, contains all the books any group of people may consider to be a part of their Bible.

Thus, a Bible reader should keep in mind the following: In a Christian Bible, The Old Testament consists of the rearranged books found in the Hebrew (Jewish) Bible. Roman Catholics and some others add some books and parts of books to that Old Testament because they were found in the Alexandrine collection. In general, Protestants do not add books to the Old Testament; they follow the Jerusalem collection of books, but rearrange them as noted above. Almost all Christians accept the twenty-seven books of the New Testament; there are a few groups who reject one or another of the books in the collection.

Thus, as you can see, this can become difficult to navigate, especially when someone says, "The Bible says . . . ." The astute Bible reader needs to ask, "Which book in which Bible says that?" There is no such thing as the original Bible. There are Bibles, various libraries of books collected over three thousand years by individuals and groups who declared their collection (canon) to be Scripture. When engaged in Bible study, it is also important to note that the Bible is a library of books written by different authors at different times in history; it is not a single book. While the authors of various books often agree with each other, there are occasions when they disagree with each other.

Presuppositions

The HB (OT) begins as stories passed on by word of mouth from one person to another. Sometime during the oral transmission stage, authors decided to collect the oral stories and write them. A change occurs immediately. One does not tell a story the same way one writes a story. Repetition and correction occur in oral story-telling. Except for future emendations by copyists, single statements by characters and plot structure dominate written stories. Furthermore, in both oral and written story-telling, types or models are employed. In the HB (OT), for example, Joshua and Elijah are types of Moses. In the CB (NT) Elizabeth becomes a type of Hannah, who is herself a type of Sarah. When orally narrating or writing a story, the teller or author consciously creates one character as a type of another to make the character and his or her words and actions intelligible to the hearer or reader.

In the CB (NT) the oldest gospel is Mark's account of Jesus' victory. The author of Matthew's Gospel copied and shortened about eighty percent of Mark's material into his book and then added other stories to make the work longer. The author of Luke's Gospel copied and shortened about fifty percent of Mark's material into his orderly account and then added other stories to make the work much longer. The material shared by Matthew and Luke is called Q—from the German word *Quelle*, meaning *Source*—by biblical scholars. Mark's Gospel begins as oral story-telling, lasting for about forty years in that form. An unidentified author, called Mark for the sake of convenience, collects the oral stories, sets a plot, and writes the first gospel around 70 CE. Because Jesus was expected to return soon, no one had thought about recording what he had said and done until Mark came along and realized that he was not returning as quickly as had been thought. About ten years after Mark finished his gospel, Matthew needed to adopt Mark's narrative—originally intended for a peasant Gentile readership—to a Jewish audience. And about twenty years after Mark finished his gospel, Luke needed to adapt Mark's poor Gentile-intended work for a rich, upper class, urban, Gentile readership. The author of John's Gospel did not know the existence of the other three works collectively named synoptic gospels. A point often overlooked by modern readers is the fact that they are not the intended readers of biblical texts. Every biblical book was written to a specific group of people at a specific time in history. Thus, Paul did not write to people living in the United States; he wrote in Greek to people living in Rome, Corinth, and Thessalonica. Modern readers are reading an English translation (and interpretation) with Roman-Greco cultural presuppositions underlying the text.

Furthermore, letters and gospels were not first intended to be read privately as is done today. They were meant to be heard in a group. The very low rate of literacy in the first century would have never dictated many copies of texts since most people could not read, and their standard practice was to listen to another read the letters and stories to them. Thus, what began as oral story-telling passed on by word of mouth became written story-telling preserved in gospels. A careful reading of Mark's Gospel will reveal the orality still embedded in the text, especially evident in the repetition of words and the organization of stories in three parts. In rewriting Mark, Matthew and Luke remove the last traces of oral story-telling.

The letters of Paul are older than the gospels. Biblical scholars divide the letters of Paul into the authentic letters—those written by Paul (Romans, Galatians, Philippians, etc.)—and those written by someone else in Paul's name—second generation Pauline letters (Ephesians, Colossians, Titus, etc.). The latter group of letters usually develop Pauline thought for a new generation of Christians. The reader of letters needs to keep in mind that the letter was not addressed to him or her; it was addressed to a specific group of believers in the mid- to late-first century CE. In addition to the Pauline body of letters, there are other letters that were gathered and placed in the CB (NT) canon (collection), such as James, 1 and 2 Peter, Jude, etc. These anonymous letters were written in the name of an apostle to give them authority in the Christian communities to which they were addressed.

Furthermore, it is important to understand that there are three different Pauls presented in the CB (NT). There is the Acts of the Apostles Paul, who is presented by the same author who wrote Luke's Gospel; in other words, Luke-Acts is a two-volume work. There is original Paul, the man who wrote or dictated letters attributed to him. And there is second-generation Paul, others who wrote under Paul's name to update some of original Paul's ideas for the next generation of believers. The caution here is to be sure that a reader is not interpreting original Paul through the lens of the Acts of the Apostles Paul. While all three Pauls are similar, their theological positions are quite different.

John Denver
Living With Grace
Spirituality

A

Never Alone

JD: Denver often sings about being never alone, never ever alone, or no one being really alone. That phrase in one form or another is found in "Love is the Master" and "It's a Possibility" on the *OW* album, in "Autograph" on the *AUTO* album, and in "On the Wings of a Dream" and "It's about Time" on the *IAT* album. *Alone* means that there is no other person nearby; however, *never* negates the meaning of the word. Thus, there is someone, who is always with us, according to Denver. In other songs, he identifies that someone as God. In "Islands" on the *SH* album, he sings about never being alone when he is visiting islands. No one wants to be looking alone for heaven or hope in "Downhill Stuff" on the *JD* album.

However, in "Seasons of the Heart" on the album with the same name, Denver sings about being most alone when lying beside the person he loves, the person with whom he has much in common, but with whom he seems to be in the process of separating. The same sentiment is expressed in "Don't Close Your Eyes Tonight" on the *DE* album; he sings about lying close to someone and still feeling all alone. Similarly, in "A Wild Heart Looking for Home" on the same album, he sings about standing in a crowd all alone. In "Sweet Misery" on the *FA* album, he sings that sweet misery is in a crowd when she is all alone. In "Looking for Space" on the *WIND* album , he finds himself all alone in the universe! It is hard to stand alone when needing someone beside one, sings Denver in "What One Man Can Do" on the *SH* album. In "Perhaps Love" on the same album, he states that when one is most alone, the memory of love will bring the other home. In "Sleepin' Alone" on the *SDD* album, Denver says that sleeping alone can make one swear to God that the night will never end, but, if the one with whom one is sleeping doesn't care, it is worse than sleeping alone.

In "Never a Doubt" on the *HG* album, Denver sings about never having a doubt that people were not meant to be lonely. In "Heart to Heart" on the *SH* album, he identifies falling in love again as being on the other side of lonely. In "Four Strong Winds" on the *FJ* album, he sings poetically about Alberta, Canada, where four strong winds blow lonely!

Scripture: "Jacob was left alone; and a man wrestled with him until daybreak. . . . [H]e said, 'Let me go, for the day is breaking.' But Jacob said, 'I will not let you go, unless you bless me.' So he said to him, 'What is your name?' and He said, 'Jacob.'" Then the man said, 'You shall no longer be called Jacob, but Israel, for you have striven with God and with humans, and have prevailed.' So Jacob called the place Peniel, saying, 'For I have seen God face to face . . . .'" (Gen 32:24, 26–28, 30, NRSV)

Reflection: At first Jacob thought he was alone. He had sent his wives and children across a stream. After he fell asleep, God appeared as a man and wrestled with him. Jacob was strong enough to pin God, who gave him the new name Israel, meaning one who strives with God. Once Jacob (Israel) realizes that he has seen God face to face, he names his campsite Peniel, which means one who has striven with divine and human beings. Thus, while he thought he was alone in his campsite, God was with Jacob. That is why Denver can sing about never being alone.

Meditation/Journal: When have you thought you were alone only to discover that God was with you?

Psalm Response: "Look at this: look / Who got picked by GOD! / He listens the split second I call to him. / At day's end I'm ready for sound sleep, / For you, GOD, have put my life back together." (Ps 4:3, 8, TM)

Autograph

JD: On the album *AUTO*, Denver records a song by the same name. In that song, he states that the songs he sings comprise his autograph. In particular, he mentions his laugh, cry, and love.

Scripture: ". . . Moses said to God, 'If I come to the Israelites and say to them, "The God of your ancestors has sent me to you," and they ask me, "What is his name?" what shall I say to them?' God said to Moses, 'I AM WHO I AM.' He said further, 'Thus you shall say to the Israelites, "I AM has sent me to you."' God also said to Moses, 'Thus you shall say to the Israelites,

"The LORD, the God of your ancestors, the God of Abraham, the God of Isaac, and the God of Jacob, has sent me to you.'"" (Exod 3:13–15a, NRSV)

Reflection: An autograph is a person's signature, one's written name on a document, such as a check, a contract, or a credit-card purchase. Denver declares that his autograph consists of the songs he sings, whereas biblically, God tells Moses that his autograph is HE WHO IS—the God who has been Abraham's, Isaac's, and Jacob's God. God's autograph also contains his name: LORD, a printed text in lieu of Yahweh (or YHWH, known as the Tetragrammaton). In other words, God's autograph is written visibly in Abraham, Isaac, and Jacob (and Moses). Parabolically, we could say that God's autograph is written with invisible ink in the same way as Denver's is written in lyrics and music.

Meditation/Journal: What is the most important document upon which you have placed your autograph? Of what did your autograph consist?

Psalm Response: "GOD, brilliant Lord, / yours is a household name. / Nursing infants gurgle choruses about you; / toddlers shout the songs . . . . / GOD, brilliant Lord, / your name echoes around the world." (Ps 8:1, 2ab, 9, TM)

B

Birds

JD: In the Denver repertoire, there are often whole songs or a line in a song that explains in depth what Denver means by the use of a word. We find that to be true in "Amazon" on the *DD* album. He sings about a bird singing his song in the jungle. In that bird's one song is found all music, and all songs are that one song. In other words, in the miniature is found the universal. For Denver the bird's song is the song of life. In "For Baby (For Bobbie)" on the *RMH* album, Denver sings about little birds singing along in time with his song expressing his love for his beloved. It is everyone's heritage to hear the songbird's call in "Children of the Universe" on the *SH* album. In "Sweet Surrender" on the *BHA* album, he compares surrender to a bird in the air. That theme is further explored in "A Wild Heart Looking for Home" on the *DE* album. Denver sings about a songbird in a cage trembling all day long as she sings as if her heart will break while watching all the free birds fly past her window. Denver urges her to forget her dreaming, to fly away, and forsake her prison-cage, because the wind still loves her. In contrast to "A Wild Heart Looking for Home" above, in "For You (Fifty Shades Freed)" on the *HG* album, Denver sings paradoxically about being free as a bird when he is flying in the cage of the person he loves.

In a few songs, Denver names specific birds. In "Catch Another Butterfly" on the *R&R* album, he names the robin. In "Children of the Universe" on the *SH* album, he names the nightingale, whippoorwill, and mourning dove. The lark is named in "Flight" on the *IAT* album, and the sparrow in "The Flower That Shattered the Stone" on the *ES* album. In "Song of Wyoming" on the *WIND* album, he sings about night birds calling and about being able to sing like a bird in a tree.

Scripture: "[Things have vanished] as, when a bird flies through the air, / no evidence of its passage is found; / the light air, lashed by the beat of its pinions / and pierced by the force of its rushing flight, / is traversed by the movement of it wings, / and afterward no sight of its coming is found there . . . ." (Wis 5:11, NRSV)

Reflection: The author of the OT (A) book of Wisdom spends time comparing the righteous to the lawless. Such things as boasting about one's wealth ultimately vanishes, like a bird's path through the air. While Denver's focus is on the bird's song, the author of Wisdom is focused on the bird's lack of leaving a trace of its path through the air, even though the air suffered the bird's flapping of its wings and its rushing from one place to another. Denver meditates on the bird's song; Wisdom reflects on its not leaving a trace of its existence.

Meditation/Journal: Take a few moments either to gaze out a window or sit outside; while doing either, listen and look for a bird. Listen to its song; watch its flight. What does it teach you about yourself?

Canticle Response: "All creatures that fly, bless the Lord; praise and honor him forever. / All beasts tame and wild, bless the Lord; praise and honor him forever. / All the offspring of the world, bless the Lord; praise and honor him forever." (Dan 3:80–82 [Sg Three 58–60], TM)

Blind

JD: In "Love Again" on the *OW* album, Denver asks what it takes for a blind man to see. His question is posed after he sings about not thinking that he would ever love again, because he was set in his ways, had given up on romance, and just figured that he would always be lonely. However, after reflecting on the fact that the eye cannot see everything, he realizes that he fell in love again, and the experience was like a blind man regaining his sight.

Scripture: "When John [the Baptist] heard in prison what the Messiah was doing, he sent word by his disciples and said to him, 'Are you the one who is to come, or are we to wait for another?' Jesus answered them, 'Go and tell John what you hear and see: the blind receive their sight, the lame walk, the lepers are cleansed, the deaf hear, the dead are raised, and the poor have good news brought to them." (Matt 11:2–5, NRSV)

Reflection: The above passage is from Q (abbreviation for Quelle), a source used by the author of Matthew's Gospel and the author of Luke's Gospel (Luke 7:22). Matthew's placement of the material serves as a summary of what precedes it. The Matthean Jesus had cured two blind men (Matt 9:27–30a). In Matthew's Gospel, Jesus is called the Messiah, which means Anointed, one called by God. In the above passage, the author of Matthew's Gospel invites his readers to answer the question: What does the restoration of sight to blind men indicate about the Messiah? In a similar manner, Denver asks: What does it take for a blind man to see? Denver's answer is that all it takes is to fall in love again, even if he didn't believe he ever would.

Meditation/Journal: What experience have you had that is like Denver's or the passage from Matthew's Gospel? Explain.

Canticle Response: "The Lord said: / On that day the deaf shall hear the words of a scroll, / and out of their gloom and darkness the eyes of the blind shall see. / The meek shall obtain fresh joy in the LORD, / and the neediest people shall exult in the Holy One . . . ." (Isa 29:13a, 18–19, NRSV)

Born Again

JD: One of Denver's crowd-favorite songs features the spiritual concept of being born again. We find it in "Rocky Mountain High" on the album by the same name. While Denver associates being born again with the season of spring in "Spring" of "Season Suite" on the *RMH* album, where he sings about the earth being reborn and life going on in spring, in "Rocky Mountain High," he sings about a twenty-seven-year-old who was born again in the summer after spending time in the mountains. All around Denver sees signs of rebirth in "Gimme Your Love" on the *DE* album; in the song, he associates rebirth with spring and defines rebirth as resurrection, renewal, and the celebration of life on earth. In "Love Is Everywhere" on the *WIND* album, he summarizes his thoughts on being born again, singing that every time someone is born again a soul is regained.

Scripture: Jesus said to Nicodemus, "'Very truly I tell you, no one can see the kingdom of God unless they are born again.' 'How can someone be born when they are old?' Nicodemus asked, 'Surely they cannot enter a second time into their mother's womb to be born!' Jesus answered, 'Very truly I tell you, no one can enter the kingdom of God unless they are born of water and the Spirit.'" (John 3:3–5, NIV)

Reflection: Sentiments like Denver's are found uniquely in John's Gospel in the CB (NT). In a dialogue with a Pharisee—traditionally an enemy of Jesus—named Nicodemus, who comes to Jesus at night to tell him that he considers Jesus to be a teacher from God. Jesus, using a double entendre, as he often does in this work, tells Nicodemus that he must be born again to see the reign of God. Like most people would, Nicodemus does not know what born again means; so, he asks Jesus how can an old person be born again: by re-entering his or her mother's womb? Literally, that is the meaning of being born again. However, the Johannine Jesus explains it metaphorically, just like Denver does. It means being born of water and the Spirit. In other words, baptism is an experience of being born again. "You must be born again," states Jesus (John 3:7, NIV). For the author of John's Gospel, as well as other CB (NT) writers, baptism is necessary to enter the reign of God. However, as Denver sings, there are other ways to be born again, such as spending time in solitude in the mountains, observing the events of the season of spring, and loving deeply.

Meditation/Journal: What have been your experiences of being born again? Make a list.

Psalm Response: "[GOD] founded Zion on the Holy Mountain— / and oh, how GOD loves his home! / Loves it far better than all / the homes of Jacob put together! / God's hometown—oh! / everyone there is talking about you! / Word's getting around; they point them out: / 'This one was born again here!' / The word's getting out on Zion: / 'Men and women, right and left, / get born again in her!' / GOD registers their names in his book: / 'This one, this one, and this one— / born again, right here.'" (Ps 87:1–3, 4b–6, TM)

C

Calypso

JD: After visiting Jacques-Yves Cousteau onboard his oceanographic ship in 1974, Denver wrote "Calypso" on the *WIND* album a year later. "Calypso" is the only Denver song to commemorate the former Royal Navy mine-sweeper that had been converted to a ferry. As a close friend of Cousteau, Denver's philosophy about the ship is contained in the line of the song about learning from the sea how to live on the land. The lyrics of the song capture the experience of sailing on a calm ocean contrasted to being in a ship-tossing storm. Denver sings about the spirit of the ship, which had become the sign of human hopes to understand nature to protect it. The music of the song features ship bells, which give the impression of rocking back and forth on the vessel, along with strings and winds, which imitate the sounds of the ocean. Both the ship and Denver's song focus on the importance of protecting the earth's natural resources, while engaging in exploration. In "Hold on Tightly" on the *IAT* album, Denver compares heartbreak to being lost in a boat on the ocean or lost in a ship at sea.

Scripture: "[Arrogance and wealth] have vanished . . . like a ship that sails through the billowy water, / and when it has passed no trace can be found, / no track of its keel in the waves. . . . [O]ne preparing to sail and about to voyage over raging waves / calls upon a piece of wood more fragile than the ship that carries him. / For it was desire for gain that planned that vessel, / and wisdom was the artisan who built it; / but it is your providence, O Father, that steers its course, / because you have given it a path in the sea, / and safe way through the waves, / showing that you can save from every danger, / so that even a person who lacks skill may put to sea. / It is your will that works of your wisdom should not be without effect; / therefore people trust their lives even to the smallest piece of wood / and passing through the billows on a raft they come safely to land." (Wis 5:9a, 10; 14:1–5, NRSV)

Reflection: The author of the OT (A) book of Wisdom reflects on the difference between the righteous and their oppressors. He concludes his meditation on the oppressors' arrogance and boasted wealth by stating that they are like a ship sailing through the sea; it leaves no impression in the water. In other words, oppressors disappear. Later in the book of Wisdom, the author reflects on the fragility of a ship on the sea, the wisdom of its designers and builders, and the providence of God to keep it safe as the waves beat against it. According to the author, people place their lives in trust of the smallest ship, because God's wisdom has been at work in the ship's building. For Denver, God's wisdom (spirit) was present in Calypso, who, in the 1970s had been transformed from top to bottom into an oceanographic vessel, and in Cousteau's crew who spread the message about the need to conserve the beauty of the seas—being strangers in their silent world, while learning from them how to live in harmony with the earth.

Meditation/Journal: What have the seas taught you about conserving earth's resources? Explain.

Psalm Response: "Some of you set sail in big ships; / you put to sea to do business in faraway ports. / Out at sea you saw GOD in action, / saw his breathtaking ways with the ocean: / With a word he called up the wind— / an ocean storm, towering waves! / You shot high in the sky, then the bottom dropped out . . . . / You were spun like a top . . . . / Then you called out to GOD in your desperate condition; / he got you out in the nick of time. / He quieted the wind down to a whisper; / put a muzzle on all the big waves. / And you were so glad when the storm died down, / and he led you safely back to harbor." (Ps 107:23–26a, 27a, 28–30, TM)

Campfire

JD: In his songs, Denver uses the element of fire in at least three ways. He sings about physical fire, like that of a campfire, around which people gather to tell stories in "Love is the Master" on the *OW* album; like sitting around the fire after supper in "Grandma's Feather Bed" on the *BHA* album; and like the slowly dying fire in the corner stove or fireplace in "Winter" of "Season Suite" on the *RMH* album. Denver also uses fire to describe the drive within a person; this is found in his wish that Montana give the subject of his song a fire in his heart in "Wild Montana Skies" on the *IAT* album; the same drive within is predicated of ponies in "Ponies" on the *DD* album, where he tells them that he has not come to steal their fire. Most people who appreciate Denver's music will remember that he calls lightning fire raining in the sky in "Rocky Mountain High" on the album of the same name. In "Perhaps Love" on the *SH* album, he proposes that love is like a fire, when it is cold. He declares that he has seen fire in "Fire and Rain" on the *PPP* album.

Scripture: ". . . Mount Sinai was wrapped in smoke, because the LORD had descended upon it in fire; the smoke went up like the smoke of a kiln, while the whole mountain shook violently." (Exod 19:18, NRSV)

Reflection: In the biblical world, fire is a sign of the divine presence. It is one of several elements of a theophany, an appearance of God. The author of the HB (OT) book of Exodus declares ". . . the appearance of the glory of the LORD was like a devouring fire on the top of the mountain . . ." (Exod 24:17, NRSV). Before Mount Sinai (Horeb) Moses experiences God as flame of fire (Exod 3:2). Among other biblical personnel who experience God as fire is Gideon in the HB (OT) book of Judges (6:11–24). God appears as fire because fire draws people to itself. The author of the CB (NT) Letter to the Hebrews states clearly: ". . . [O]ur God is a consuming fire" (Heb 12:29). That is what Denver experienced around a campfire, near a fireplace or stove, as lightning, and as the inner drive that keeps people keeping on. Fire is a spiritual experience that Denver shares with those who love his songs.

Psalm Response: "GOD, my God, how great you are! / beautifully, gloriously robed. / Dressed up in sunshine, / and all heaven stretched out for your tent. / You built your palace on the ocean deeps, / made a chariot out of clouds and took off on wind-wings. / You commandeered winds as messengers, / appointed fire and flame as ambassadors." (Ps 104:1b–4, TM)

Circle

JD: A circle is a perfect hollow ring; it is a curved line surrounding a center point with every point of the line being an equal distance from the center point. In other words, a circle is inclusive; it encompasses all. That is why Denver refers to the circle of life in "The Wings that Fly Us Home" on the *SP* album. The opening lyrics declare that in the circle called life, there are many ways of being. Later in his song-philosophical reflection, he sings about love being all that is infinite in one. That is why in "Love is Everywhere" on the *WIND* album, he issues an invitation to dance in the circle of love and light. It is also why in "Whalebones and Crosses" on the *AUTO* album that he sings about the circle of the mighty spirit who keeps both the living and the dead in the human fold.

Scripture: "[Job said: God] has inscribed a circle on the surface of the waters / At the boundary of light and darkness." (Job 26:10, NASB)

Reflection: The above verse from the HB (OT) book of Job reflects the first creation account found in the HB (OT) book of Genesis. To tame chaos, God marks a circle on the abyss (outer space) to separate light and darkness. In other words, God contains the waters of chaos with a circle on the horizon, where light and darkness meet. His circumscription of waters and separation of light and darkness are familiar features of the first Genesis creation account (Gen 1:4–7). While Denver wants to draw circles that include, according to biblical texts, God draws circles that exclude.

Meditation/Journal: In your lifetime, what circles have you drawn? How does each include? How does each exclude? Into what circles have you been drawn? Did they include or exclude? Explain.

Psalm Response: "Truly God is good to the upright, / to those who are pure in heart. / But as for me, my feet had almost stumbled; / my steps had nearly slipped. / For I was envious of the arrogant; / I saw the prosperity of the wicked. / If I had said, 'I will talk on in this way,' / I would have been untrue to the circle of your children. / . . . [F]or me it is good to be near God; / I have made the Lord GOD my refuge, / to tell of all your works." (Ps 73:1–3, 15, 28, NRSV)

[B] Clouds

JD: Because of his mountain climbing experiences, Denver knew that there are times when climbing a mountain that a person rises above the clouds around a mountain or can see the clouds forming lower than the summit in the distance. He reflects those experiences in "Rocky Mountain High" on the album of the same name, when he sings about a twenty-seven-year-old man who sees silver clouds below the summit. Mountain climbers know that clouds signal storms approaching; storms may consist of rain, sleet, snow, thunder, and lightning. That phenomenon is reflected in "Ponies" on the *DD* album, where Denver sings about storm clouds gathering in the west and the ponies, hearing the thunder, are getting ready to run wild before it rains. In "Perhaps Love" on the *SH* album, Denver sings about love being like a cloud; while he doesn't explain what he means, from the rest of the song we can infer that the love of another involves relationship storms, and, that like a cloud, they form and disappear. In "Sticky Summer Weather" on the *TMT* album, he compares dreaming to the sun hiding behind a cloud.

Scripture: ". . . [T]he LORD said to Moses, 'I am going to come to you in a dense cloud . . . .' On the morning of the third day there was thunder and lightning, as well as a thick cloud on the mountain . . . ." (Exod 19:9, 16, NRSV)

Reflection: Throughout both the HB (OT) and the CB (NT), a cloud is a sign of the divine presence. It appears not only on Mount Sinai (Horeb), but over the tent of meeting (Exod 33:10–11a). It fills the tabernacle (Exod 40:34). The cloud appears in all three versions of Jesus' transfiguration (Mark 9:7; Matt 17:5; Luke 9:34). Often referred to as a pillar of cloud, it reveals the glory of the LORD (Exod 13:21), and it signifies the divine presence in the Jerusalem Temple (1 Kgs 8:10b–11; 2 Chr 5:14). Many other references to the cloud as a sign of the divine presence abound in both the HB (OT) and the CB (NT). Because the Hebrews, Israelites, Jews, and early Christians thought that their gods lived on mountain tops, like other religious people did, a cloud on a mountain indicated that the LORD God was present there.

Meditation/Journal: What does a cloud represent for you? Explain.

Psalm Response: "[GOD] steps down [from heaven]; / under his feet an abyss opens up. / He's riding a winged creature, / swift on wind-wings. / Now he's wrapped himself / in a trenchcoat of black-cloud darkness. / But his cloud-brightness bursts through, / spraying hailstones and fireballs." (Ps 18:9–12, TM)

D

Dance

JD: The word *dance* is not one that Denver uses often in his songs. However, on the *AUTO* album he recorded "Dancing with the Mountains." In that song he sings about catching what he calls dancing fever, a reference to dancing to rock-and-roll music. He declares that dancing can make one whole, and he states that he dances with the mountains, the wind, and on the ocean. Later in the song, he sings about everyone being one when dancing with the mountains. In "Poems, Prayers and Promises" on the album with the same name, he says that he would like to dance across the mountains on the moon. Usually, dance, refers to moving one's feet and body rhythmically to music and, usually, in time to music; however, for Denver dance suggests experiencing spiritual unity not only with nature (mountains, wind, ocean), but also with other people. Such is the case with "Dance Little Jean" on the *FJ* album. In the song, Denver narrates how wedding guests observe a little girl named Jean dancing and how they were all drawn in as they watched her on the dance floor. As the song progresses, the listeners discover that little Jean is dancing for joy because it is her mother's and father's wedding! In his tribute to Christa McAuliffe and the rest of the crew of the Space Shuttle Challenger that exploded after takeoff in 1986 killing all seven crew members onboard, he sings about wanting to dance on a falling star, after wishing on the Milky Way in "Flying for Me" on the *OW* album. Many people do not know that Denver was a candidate to be the first civilian in space, but he was unable to join the mission, and, so, McAuliffe was selected in his place. In the song, he sings about her (McAuliffe) flying for him and everyone; she gave her light, spirit, and life to the mission.

Scripture: "It was told King David, 'The LORD has blessed the household of Obed-edom and all that belongs to him, because of the ark of God.' So David went and brought up the ark of God from the house of Obed-edom to the city of David with rejoicing . . . . David danced before the LORD with all his might; David was girded with a linen ephod." (2 Sam 6:12, 14, NRSV)

Reflection: Like Denver's music, the Bible is poor when it comes to dance; and when it does mention dance, it often leads to something undesirable, like the beheading of John the Baptist (Mark 6:17–29; Matt 14:1–12). David's dance before God's ark, as it is being carried in procession to Jerusalem, receives criticism from his wife Michal, who, after watching the spectacle occur, tells him that she thinks he has dishonored himself as King of Israel by dancing with only a linen apron covering his body. David replies that he danced before the LORD because God made him king (2 Sam 6:20–23). Bringing the ark from the home of Obed-edom, where it had been kept for a time, was a political move for the young king. After he had taken Jerusalem from its former occupiers and made it his capital city, he strengthened his position by bringing a sign of God's presence to his city. Thus, everyone could see that God was on his side! And this occurred while he was dancing with abandon before the LORD. The dance, like that sung about by Denver, spiritually united the people of his kingdom.

Meditation/Journal: What does dance mean or signify to you? Explain.

Psalm Response: "Hallelujah! / Praise God in his holy house of worship, / praise him under the open skies; / Praise him for his acts of power, / praise him for his magnificent greatness; / Praise him with castanets and dance . . . . / Let every living, breathing creature praise GOD! / Hallelujah!" (Ps 150:1–2, 4a, 6, TM)

Dawn

JD: In a not-too-well-known Denver song on the *SP* album, named "In the Grand Way," the author sings about finding perfect harmonies while standing in the dawn of a new day about to arrive. He adds that he is not looking for a tomorrow. This love song is about a new experience of love with hope (dawn) and the first time loving the morning. In "Late Nite Radio" on the *WIND* album, he acknowledges the lonely hearts of truckers, who are kept company in the early morning, specifically between midnight and dawn, by late night radio broadcasts on the national airwaves. As in "In the Grand Way," dawn in "Late Nite Radio" represents hope, specifically for those who are lonely.

Scripture: "On the seventh day [Joshua, the priests, and the armed guard] rose early, at dawn, and marched around the city [of Jericho] . . . seven times. As soon as the people heard the sound of the trumpets, they raised a great shout, and the wall fell down flat; so that the people charged straight ahead into the city and captured it." (Josh 6:15, 20b, NRSV)

Reflection: Dawn is a time of hope, as Denver sings, in biblical literature. Joshua, who succeeded Moses as leader of the Israelites, instructs the priests carrying the ark of God and the armed guard to march around the city of Jericho one time for six successive days in order to conquer it. However, on the seventh day they marched around it seven times, and, with a shout, the wall fell. All the marching took place at dawn, as a new day is beginning. They march around it seven times on the seventh day because seven is the sum of three—the biblical number for God—and four—the biblical number for earth. Moses had stretched out his hand over the sea, and the LORD drove it back by a strong east wind all night (Exod 14:21). Then, after the Israelites had walked through the sea, Moses stretch out his hand over it again, and at dawn the sea returned to its normal depth, drowning the Egyptians who had followed the Israelites into the sea's space (Exod 14:27–28). Thus, at dawn, God destroyed Israel's enemy, just like, at dawn, he made it possible for Joshua to capture Jericho. The dawn of a new day gives people hope.

Meditation/Journal: What do you consider to be important experiences of your life that occurred at dawn? Make a list.

Psalm Response: "My heart, O God, is steadfast; / I will sing and make music with all my soul. / Awake, harp and lyre! / I will awaken the dawn. / I will praise you, LORD, among the nations; / I will sing of you among the peoples. / For great is your love, higher than the heavens; / your faithfulness reaches to the skies." (Ps 108:1–4, NIV)

Doors

JD: In "Perhaps Love" on the *GH3* album, Denver sings about love being like an open door, which invites one to come closer and to see. In "Love Again" on the *GH3* album, he sings about thinking that he would never love again; thus, the metaphor he used was locked doors. That metaphor is also used in "We Don't Live Here No More" on the *FA* album. This song is full of oxymoronic statements, like building a house without doors. A door is a type of portal to somewhere else, if one chooses to walk through it and experience whatever is there; that is why Denver compares love to an open door. However, when someone thinks that he or she will never love again, a person moves into a house with a locked door or a home with no doors at all. No one can get in, and no one can get out through the portal.

Scripture: Moses said to the elders of Israel: "Go, select lambs for your families, and slaughter the passover lamb. Take a bunch of hyssop, dip it in the blood that is in the basin, and touch the lintel and the two doorposts with the blood in the basin. None of you shall go outside the door of your house until morning." (Exod 12:21–22, NRSV)

Reflection: The directions for celebrating the first Passover found in the HB (OT) book of Exodus is focused on the door of Israelite houses. After killing a spring lamb, its blood is to be collected in a basin; blood is sacred to the Israelites, because they believe that life is contained in it. Thus, when any animal is slain, its blood is poured into the earth; once the Temple was built in Jerusalem, the blood was splashed on an altar and from there flowed into the earth. While the blood on the doors of the Israelites protects their lives, the slaughtered lamb represents the death of the firstborn Egyptians and livestock (Exod 12:29). In other words, the blood on the doorposts blocked the LORD's entry through the portal. Once the death of the firstborn of the Egyptians was accomplished, the Egyptians told Moses and the Israelites to open their doors and leave Egypt.

Meditation/Journal: To whom or what have you recently closed your door? Explain. To whom or what have you recently opened your door? Explain.

Psalm Response: "Lift up your heads, you gates; / be lifted up, you ancient doors, / that the King of glory may come in. / Who is this King of glory? / The LORD strong and mighty, / the LORD mighty in battle. / Lift up your heads, you gates; / lift them up, you ancient doors, / that the King of glory may come in. / Who is he, this King of glory? / The LORD Almighty— / he is the King of glory." (Ps 24:7–10, NIV)

Dream

JD: Denver uses the word *dream* in multiple songs and uses it with its variety of meanings. First, a dream can be some kind of imagining while one sleeps. Such is the experience Denver expresses in "Shanghai Breezes" on the *GH3* album; he tells the person from whom he is separated that she is in his dreams, and, as such, is always near him. In "Thanks to You" on *FTSS* album, he declares that he was going nowhere; he was a man without a dream. However, he looked into his beloved's eyes and dreamed about forever.

Second, a dream can be a waking imagining, something one is considering, as in "Along for the Ride ('55 T-Bird)" on the *OW* album, in which Denver sings about his desire to have someone sitting beside him in his T-Bird with the top down; oxymoronically, he called it a convertible dream! In a similar way, on the *IAT* album in "On the Wings of a Dream" he considers the shortness of life. After singing about having a dream during the night about dying and being buried, he reflects on how fast we disappear. In "Sing Australia" on the *HG* album, he mentions the aboriginal legends of dream time. On the *SH* album, there are several songs that mention waking imagining. In "Seasons of the Heart," Denver sings that love is still the only dream he knows. In "Dreams" he sings about dreams that sail away on the sea, dreams in need of company, and dreams that stay inside all day. He swears to the one he loves that if dreams come true, he will dream of his beloved that night. He also mentions a man who dreams of his reward; he concludes by stating that he thinks people are afraid to dream. In "Relatively Speaking," on the *SH* album, he tells the one he loves that she is living his dream. In "What One Man Can Do" on the same album, he states that one man can dream, while in "Islands" on the *SH* album, Denver dreams of home, where he is never alone, and then he compares dreams to uninhabited islands,

Third, the word dream can refer to something for which one hopes or wishes, as in "Rocky Mountain Suite" on the *FA* album. Denver philosophizes that tomorrow is one of yesterday's dreams. Likewise, in "Dreamland Express" on the album with the same name—where most of the songs have some dreamy aspect to them—he sings about not being able to believe or conceive that his dream would come true. Yet, in "Higher Ground" on the album with the same name, he sings about the possibility of living his dream. In "Fly Away" on the *WIND* album, he sings about a woman whose dreams have dried or flown away. Likewise, he sings about a soldier, who, to be his best, dreamed about being a good comrade, in "Let Us Begin (What are we Making Weapons for?)" on the *OW* album. Also on the *OW* album is Denver's tribute to the crew of the Challenger—"Flying for Me"—in which he expresses his desire to carry the dreams of all people into space and, if given the chance, people who dream can explore space. In "On the Wings of an Eagle" on the *FJ* album, he sings that he can dream of friendly skies. He acknowledges that it is easy to lose a dream or hope for the future in "It's a Possibility" on *the OW* album, which uses the word *dream* in many of the lyrics of the songs on the album. In "Take Me to Tomorrow" on the album with the same name, he asks his listeners about their dreams—their plans or schemes. After addressing a caged songbird in "A Wild Heart Looking for Home" on the *DE* album, he sings that dreaming of freedom will not fit in a cage; then, he urges the songbird to follow its dream of flying to heaven. In "Dance Little Jean" on the *FJ* album, he sings about a little girl on a dance floor and how all the guests watched her and were drawn into her dream. Also on the *FJ* album is "Nobody Can Take My Dreams from Me." In that song Denver mentions both dreams of flying and dreams of being free—dreams which no one can take from him .

Fourth, Denver uses the word *dream* in its daydream aspect, namely, letting the mind dwell on pleasant scenes and images while awake. In "Love Again" on the *OW* album, he expresses that idea when he says he often thinks that he is dreaming, when he considers falling in love again. Likewise, in "Around and Around" on the *PPP* album, he sings about dreams that are full of promises and dreams he cannot remember. In "What's on Your Mind" on the *JD* album, he reflects that he has seen love face to face in his dreams. In "Seasons of the Heart" on the album with the same name, he declares that love is the only dream he knows. However, in "Sticky Summer Weather" on the *TMT* album, he sings about a time, he thinks, when he remembers dreaming. In "A Baby Just Like You" on the *ACT* album, he tells his son, Zachary, that he has set Denver's soul to dreaming, and near the end of the song, he offers a wish, a dream, that his son will know the warmth of love.

Scripture: The LORD said to Moses, Aaron, and Miriam: "Hear my words: When there are prophets among you, / I the LORD make myself known to them in visions; / I speak to them in dreams. / Not so with my servant Moses; / he is entrusted with all my house. / With him I speak face to face—clearly, not in riddles; / and he beholds the form of the LORD." (Num 12:6–8a, NRSV)

Reflection: The passage above from the HB (OT) book of Numbers emphasizes Moses' authority; according to the author, he outranks prophets, Aaron (his brother), and Miriam (his sister). God speaks face to face with Moses, but he delivers his messages to prophets in visions and dreams. One of the best biblical prophets is Daniel, who not only dreams, but interprets others' dreams. In the HB (OT) book of Genesis, there is Joseph, son of Jacob, identified as a dreamer, who is also able to interpret others' dreams. The author of the CB (NT) gospel of Matthew presents Joseph, husband of Mary, as a dreamer, modeled after his HB (OT) namesake. As stated in the book of Numbers, ancient people believed that God spoke to and revealed himself to them in their dreams. Using all the modern interpretations of dreams, Denver reveals that he thinks the same in his songs.

Meditation/Journal: In what form (asleep, waking, hope, daydream) do you dream the most? Explain. What do you interpret your dreams to mean?

Psalm Response: "A long time ago you [, GOD,] spoke in a vision, / you spoke to your faithful beloved: / I've crowned a hero, / I chose the best I could find; / I found David, my servant, / poured holy oil on his head, / And I'll keep my hand steadily on him, / yes, I'll stick with him through thick and thin." (Ps 89:19–22, TM)

Dying

JD: As already noted above, Denver sings about dreaming about dying in "On the Wings of a Dream" on the *IAT* album. In that song, he expresses his thought that the present moment is the only thing we own. We are here for only that moment, and then we are gone soon. He also mentions that the body leaves us, implying that there is more to us than just a body. In "I'm Sorry" on the *WIND* album, he expresses his sorrow at being alone again due to a breakup of some kind. He says that he is sorry for himself for lies, unsaid things, and for taking the other for granted. His sorrow is so deep that he sings about dying down deep inside. While the first kind of dying, the physical, awaits all creation, the second kind of dying, emotional, means that he feels like he is dying.

Scripture: ". . . [W]e have this treasure [ministry] in clay jars, so that it may be made clear that this extraordinary power belongs to God and does not come from us. We are . . . always carrying in the body the death of Jesus, so that the life of Jesus may also be made visible in our bodies. For while we live, we are always being given up to death for Jesus' sake, so that the life of Jesus may be made visible in our mortal flesh. . . . [A]s servants of God we have commended ourselves in every way . . . . We are treated . . . as dying, and see—we are alive . . . ." (2 Cor 4:7, 10–11; 6:4, 8b–9, NRSV)

Reflection: In his Second Letter to the Corinthians in the CB (NT), Paul relays that he has experienced a type of dying, just like Denver does. He interprets the dying he experiences in his ministry to the Gentiles as a way God's power is manifested paradoxically in a spiritual sense. In the experience of dying, he is more alive than ever; dying reveals the life of Jesus in Paul's dying flesh. Those who are buried with the Anointed One (Jesus) in baptism are also raised to life with Christ (Rom 6:3–4). To be united with Christ for Paul means that the minister will suffer and die as Jesus did; through participation in the sufferings of Jesus, one attains the resurrection of the dead, like Christ did (Phil 3:10–11). In other words, in the midst of experiencing dying, life is present spiritually. And this is what Denver sings about in several songs; one song is about dying inside because of the loss of a relationship, and another is about the life found in a new relationship.

Meditation/Journal: When have you most recently experienced dying inside? Explain. How long after that experience did you discover life again?

Psalm Response: "I sing to GOD, the Praise-Lofty, / and find myself safe and saved. / The hangman's noose was tight at my throat; / devil waters rushed over me. / Hell's ropes cinched me tight; / death traps barred every exit. / A hostile world! I call to GOD, / I cry to God to help me. / From his palace he hears my call; / my cry brings me right into his presence / a private audience!" (Ps 18:3–6, TM)

E

Eagle

JD: In the "Eagle and the Hawk"—which is more about the hawk than the eagle—on the *AER* album, Denver identifies the eagle as a bird who inhabits the high country. As anyone who has watched an eagle in flight knows, it sores on air currents while looking for food. As Denver sings, watching an eagle in flight gives the viewer a feeling of freedom. For a man like Denver, who loved to fly, the eagle reminded him of soaring on air currents in a plane—almost touching mountain tops while looking at canyons below. In "Looking for Space" on the *WIND* album, Denver again compares the experience of flying to seeing an eagle soaring in the sky. The eagle's freedom represents hope for the future, that people will be all that they can be spiritually and not remain on the plateau where they are. In "Rocky Mountain High" on the album with the same name, Denver sings that the twenty-seven-year-old, who discovered his spirituality while hiking and climbing in the Rocky Mountains, would be a poor man if he never saw an eagle fly. In "Flight (The Higher We Fly)" on the *IAT* album, Denver recounts flying high, where even eagles do not go. He sings that he is one with wind and eagles in "On the Wings of An Eagle" on the *FJ* album. In "Eagles & Horses" on *FTSS* album, he sings about a vision of eagles and horses; he explains that eagles inhabit heavenly heights and know neither limit nor bound, just as he has experienced in a plane. He calls them the guardian angels of light and dark; they see all, and they hear every sound. He concludes that his spirit is like the eagle.

Scripture: "[The LORD] sustained [his people] in a desert land, / in a howling wilderness waste; / he shielded [them], cared for [them], / guarded [them] as the apple of his eye. / As an eagle stirs up its nest, / and hovers over its young; / as it spreads its wings, takes them up, / and bears them aloft on its pinions, / the LORD alone guided [them] . . . ." (Deut 32:10–12a, NRSV)

Reflection: In biblical literature, the eagle appears first in the HB (OT) book of Exodus. After leading the Israelites out of Egypt and arriving at Mount Horeb (Sinai), Moses ascends the mountain and the LORD tells him to tell the Israelites, "You have seen what I did to the Egyptians, and how I bore you on eagles' wings and brought you to myself" (Exod 19:4, NRSV). The metaphor is God is like an eagle; in other words, he carried his chosen people to freedom. That image is expanded in the Scripture above from the HB (OT) book of Deuteronomy. There God is depicted as one who sustained his people in the wilderness; like an eagle he watched over his people and, like eagle parents teach their fledglings how to fly, when it is time for them to leave the nest, God guided his people through the desert. Denver's focus on the freedom of the eagle in flight is found in the fact that the LORD provided for the Israelites' escape from Egyptian slavery to freedom in the land promised to Abraham and his descendants.

Meditation/Journal: If you have seen an eagle fly, what emotions did the experience evoke in you? If you have never seen an eagle fly, what do you think the experience of watching an eagle soar on wind currents evokes in people?

Psalm Response: "Praise the LORD . . . ; / all my inmost being, praise his holy name. / Praise the LORD . . . , / and forget not all his benefits— / who forgives all your sins / and heals all your diseases, / who redeems your life from the pit / and crowns you with love and compassion, / who satisfies your desires with good things / so that your youth is renewed like the eagle's." (Ps 103:1–5, NIV)

Earth

JD: In "The Flower that Shattered the Stone" on the *ES* album—a whole album of songs considered to be earth songs—Denver sings about the earth, spinning on its axis, being our mother. Also, in "Boy from the Country" on the *AEJD* album, the boy from the country calls the earth his mother. The earth is mother of all in "American Child" on the *AUTO* album, while in "It's About Time" on the album with the same name, Denver sings that it is about time to understand that the earth is the only home people have. The green earth below is the one world for all people in "The One World," the 1988 Theme Song for the Global Forum. While he doesn't use the word *earth* in "Joseph & Joe" on the *JD* album, he does sing about mother (earth) teaching what people need to learn.

In "Flying for Me" on the *OW* album, he refers to the earth as a space-ship. Feeling warm earth is something that grandpa misses in "Wild Flowers in a Mason Jar (The Farm)" on the *SDD* album. Earth—referred to as clay—is the substance used by the potter on his wheel in "Potter's Wheel" on the *DD* album. In "Spring," part of the "Season Suite" on the *RMH* album, is the time when the earth is reborn and life goes on. During spring—in April—people celebrate earth day, and Denver sings about making earth day a celebration every day in "Earth Day Every Day (Celebrate)" on the *ES* album. In "Dancing with the Mountains" on the *GH3* album, Denver asks the listener if he or she were present when the earth stood still. From a biblical point of view, it is not the earth that stood still, but the sun stood still (Josh 10:13; Sir 46:4). In "Ancient Rhymes" on *FTSS* album, Denver welcomes a precious earth-made child, and in "Falling Leaves (The Refugees)" on the *HG* album, he desires one wish on earth, namely, to bless the falling leaves (the refugees).

Scripture: "Moses was keeping the flock of his father-in-law . . . and came to Horeb, the mountain of God. There the angel of the LORD appeared to him in a flame of fire out of a bush; he looked, and the bush was blazing, yet it was not consumed. Then Moses said, 'I must turn aside to see why the bush is not burned up.' When the LORD saw that he had turned aside to see, God called to him out of the bush, 'Moses, Moses! Come no closer! Remove the sandals from your feet, for the place on which you are standing is holy ground.'" (Exod 3:1–5, NRSV)

Reflection: In the HB (OT), another name for Mount Horeb is Sinai, otherwise called the mountain of God in biblical literature. The Hebrews (Israelites, Jews), like all other ancient people, believe that their God, the LORD, lived on the top of a mountain, because a mountain reached from the middle level of their three-storied universe—where people lived—to the top level—where God lived. However, the fire that gets Moses' curiosity is a sign of the LORD's presence on earth. And that presence—often referred to biblically as the angel of the LORD—makes the earth holy or sacred.

Because Joshua, Moses' successor, is portrayed biblically as a new Moses, he encounters "the commander of the army of the LORD" (Josh 5:14, NRSV), who tells him to remove his sandals because the place where he stands is holy (Josh 5:15). The holy-ground incident is remembered in the CB (NT) in a long speech delivered by Stephen (Acts 7:33). Denver uses a modern, scientific understanding of the earth as being one planet among others rotating on its own axis while also rotating around the sun to celebrate its holiness or sacredness; that is why he calls it our mother, reborn in spring, that is not only the substance on potters' wheels spun into ceramics, but the very holy substance of which people are made (Gen 2:7) and upon which they walk and touch.

Meditation/Journal: In what specific ways do you treat the earth as holy or sacred?

Psalm Response: "Be good to me, God—and now! / I've run to you for dear life. / I'm hiding out under your wings . . . . / I call out to High God, / the God who holds me together. / God delivers generous love, / he makes good on his word. / Soar high in the skies, O God! / Cover the whole earth with your glory!" (Ps 57:1–2, 3b, 5, TM)

Eyes

JD: In his songs, Denver uses eyes in singing about reading or interpreting the physical eyes of others, once his eyes have been opened in "Till You Opened My Eyes" on the *SDD* album. In "True Love Takes Time" on the *OW* album, he sings about traveling on a road and waiting for the moment when his eyes would see. In "The Flower That Shattered the Stone" on the *ES* album, he desires to see with his own eyes the pure love growing in the hearts of children, while in "River" on the *FJ* album, he says he can see the cold morning in the river's eyes.

In "Come and Let Me Look in Your Eyes" on the *SP* album, he invites others to come and let him look in their eyes, because, as he sings in "Hitchhiker" on the *SP* album, the eyes tell one where another has been. They also tell what is hard to believe, as in "Berkeley Woman" on the *JD* album; his eyes showed him her cheek color and her natural skin tone. Also, he saw the hurt in her eyes. Likewise, in "Autograph" on the album with the same name, Denver sings about closing his eyes in an attempt not to see all that he is seeing; later in the song he opens his eyes, saying that love in the eyes of the others is what he would like to see.

On the *HG* album in "For You (Fifty Shades Freed)," he sings about being alive in the other's eyes and knowing he was there—seeing it in the other's eyes. He likes ladies with big brown eyes in "Deal with the Ladies" on the *HG* album. Remembering a wonderful weekend with another in "Thought of You" on the *IAT* album, Denver says that the thought brings tears to his eyes. He sings about hiding behind his eyes in "On the Wings of an Eagle" on the *FJ* album, states that his eyes cannot take the sun in "To the Wild Country" on the *ES* album, and that the light in his beloved's eyes makes him warm in "Back Home Again" on the album with the same name. In the words of "Love Again" on the *GH3* album, there may be more than what meets the eye. He seems to identify what the more is in "The Flower That Shattered the Stone" on the *ES* album, asking if there is someone with halloes in his or her eyes. In "Wild Montana Skies" on the *GH3* album, he asks the state of Montana to give light to the eyes of a man born in the Bitterroot Valley. And in "Love is Everywhere" on the *WIND* album, Denver exhorts his listeners to open their eyes to both joy and pain.

Scripture: "Ah, you are beautiful my love; / ah, you are beautiful, / your eyes are doves. / How beautiful you are, my love, / how very beautiful! / Your eyes are doves / behind your veil. / His eyes are like doves, / beside springs of water, bathed in milk, / fitly set. / Turn away your eyes from me, / for they overwhelm me! / Your eyes are pools . . . ." (Song 1:15; 4:1; 5:12; 6:5; 7:4, NRSV)

Reflection: In the verses above from the HB (OT) book of the Song of Songs, the love poem switches from verses about the female partner to the male partner. Both compare each other's eyes to doves. The meaning is that the almond shape of the eyes is like the shape of a dove's body; the eyes are bright, shiny black, like a dove's eyes, or they are like the gray-blue color of a dove's eyes; the woman's fluttering eyelashes remind the man of a dove's fluttering wings. Doves, of course, were signs of love throughout the world. The woman's eyes are also like pools of water sparkling in the sunshine. There, moistness causes them to shine or sparkle; the man declares that the woman's eyes dazzle him; they have power over him in the same way that Denver sings about eyes.

Meditation/Journal: How would you describe your eyes? Choose your spouse or a friend and gaze into his or her eyes; what do you see?

Psalm Response: "God-friendship is for God-worshipers; / They are the ones he confides in. / If I keep my eyes on GOD, / I won't trip over my own feet. / Look at me and help me! / I'm all alone and in big trouble. / Keep watch over me and keep me out of trouble; / Don't let me down when I run to you." Ps 25:14–16, 20, TM)

F

Field

JD: The best source for Denver's use of the word field is in "Let Us Begin (What Are We Making Weapons For?)" on the *OW* album. In that song, Denver sings about the son of a grassland farmer, who, like the four generations of his forebears, worked the land and left blood in the topsoil on the farmland. In "Mother Nature's Son" on the *RMH* album, he sings about a young country boy who can be found in a field of grass, and in "Zachary and Jennifer" on the *FA* album, he sings about Jennifer who will dance in fields of flowers. Thus, for Denver a field can be a part of a farm, a pasture of grass, or a high-country meadow where wildflowers thrive.

Scripture: "[Two disciples] brought [a] colt to Jesus and thew their cloaks on it, and he sat on it. Many people spread their cloaks on the road, and others spread leafy branches that they had cut in the fields. Then those who went ahead and those who followed were shouting, 'Hosanna! / Blessed is the one who comes in the name of the Lord! / Blessed is the coming kingdom of our ancestor David! / Hosanna in the highest heaven!'" (Mark 11:7–10, NRSV)

Reflection: In general, a field is an area of open ground, especially an area used to grow crops or graze livestock. With that understanding, one could ask where people found leafy branches to cut in the fields in Mark's Gospel? The author of Matthew's Gospel omits the description of people going into the fields to cut branches and simply states that they cut branches from trees (Matt 21:8), and the author of Luke's Gospel is focused only on cloaks on the road (Luke 19:36). In John's Gospel, people take branches of palm trees to wave before Jesus; this note in John's Gospel is what gives the name of Palm Sunday—more accurately named Cloak Sunday—to the Sunday one week before Easter Sunday. Since a field is an open or uncluttered space, the author of Mark's Gospel uses the word *field* like Denver does: to indicate an open area of land with grass or flowers.

Meditation/Journal: What extraordinary experiences have you had in a field? Choose one and narrate it.

Psalm Response: "Offer prayers unceasing to [God], / bless him from morning to night. / Fields of golden grain in the land, / cresting the mountains in wild exuberance, / Cornucopias of praise, praises / springing from the city like grass from the earth. / May he never be forgotten, / his fame shine on like sunshine. / May all . . . people enter his circle of blessing / and bless the One who blessed them." (Ps 72:15b–17, TM)

Find Self

JD: While the phrase is not used extensively in Denver's songs, the desire to find one's self is, nevertheless, a prominent theme. It can be found on the *SP* album in "Come and Let Me Look in Your Eyes." Denver sings that all he wants to do is to try and find himself, because he acknowledges that he seems to be lost on his way. On the *WIND* album in "Looking for Space," he is on the road of experience looking for space to find out who he is. There are times, he sings, when things are clear—especially when he is in the sunshine and in his dreams. He advises his listeners that when they are looking for space to find out who they are that answers are hard to find. The twenty-seven-year-old in "Rocky Mountain High" on the album with the same name keeps changing fast, and the change does not last long. The agent of his change is his sight that has turned inside himself to help him understanding serenity and fill his life with wonder. In other words, insight has helped him to find himself. In "To the Wild Country" on the *ES* album, Denver sings about having the fear that he will lose himself and not know who he is, as he gets caught in struggles and strains. In "Perhaps Love" on the *SH* album, he sings that even if one loses self and does not know what to do, the memory of love will see the person through the experience.

Scripture: "I [, the Teacher,] said to myself, 'I have acquired great wisdom, surpassing all who were over Jerusalem before me; and my mind has had great experience of wisdom and knowledge.' And I applied my mind to know wisdom and to know madness and folly. I perceived that this also is but a chasing after wind." (Eccl 1:16–17, NRSV)

Reflection: The Teacher—otherwise known as Qoheleth—reflects on vanity; in Hebrew the word means *vapor* or *wind*, things transient and impermanent. While the Teacher has acquired great wisdom and knowledge, he reflects (in his mind) upon those who chase after the wind; this means that they can never reach achievement totally; they are a futile exertion of energy. Similarly, attempting to find one's self is a chase after wind, because the self changes with the passing of years. Finding oneself, as Denver sings about the process, is a lifetime journey of self-discovery that involves exploring values, passions, strengths, and weaknesses to gain a deeper understanding of one's authentic self. When having a good definition of self, a person can make decisions that align with his or her values, passions, and purpose. Like the Teacher, embracing one's unique story and living according to it gives one a deeper understanding of self and sets one free to be who he or she is. Knowing self gives one a strong sense of self-confidence, which radiates in interactions with others and empowers one to take risks, pursue dreams, and overcome challenges in life. For this to occur a person needs insight about himself or herself to find out who he or she is.

Meditation/Journal: Who are you? Prepare a definition of your true or authentic self?

Psalm Response: "GOD, I'm not trying to rule the roost, / I don't want to be king of the mountain. / I haven't meddled where I have no business / or fantasized grandiose plans. / I've kept my feet on the ground, / I've cultivated a quiet heart. / Like a baby content in its mother's arms, / my soul is a baby content." (Ps 131:1–2, TM)

Friend

JD: Because the word *friend* can refer to someone who is emotionally close to another, someone who has a close personal relationship of mutual affection and trust with another, someone who has a casual relationship with another (acquaintance), someone who is an ally (non-enemy), someone who defends or supports a cause, or someone who supports a charity or institution (patron), all that can be done here is give a few examples of how Denver uses the word in his songs. On the *AUTO* album, he uses the word friend in four different songs. In "Dancing with the Mountains," Denver declares that his dancing partners are more than friends. In "The Ballad of St. Anne's Reel," he sings about a new friend and a welcomed friend. In "In My Heart," he watches his best friend leave, while in "Song for the Life," he sings for the friend he has found. The twenty-seven-year-old in "Rocky Mountain High," on the album with the same name, loses a friend but keeps his memory, while in "Goodbye Again," Denver sings about having to leave and see some friends. Late night radio is his best friend when he is lonely in "Late Nite Radio" on the *WIND* album. He sings about both living and dying being one's most intimate friends in "We Don't Live Here No More" on the *FA* album. On the *IAT* album, in "On the Wings of a Dream," he declares that there are people in this life who are friends from our heavenly home. After singing that his body is merely the shell of his soul in "Eagles & Horses" on *FTSS* album, he compares that statement to an old friend who had been tried and been true.

Scripture: ". . . Moses used to take the tent and pitch it outside the camp, far off from the camp; he called it the tent of meeting. When Moses entered the tent, the pillar of cloud would descend and stand at the entrance of the tent, and the LORD would speak with Moses. Thus the LORD used to speak to Moses face to face, as one speaks to a friend." (Exod 33:7a, 9, 11a, NRSV)

Reflection: There is no single definition for the word *friend*. As seen above, Denver uses it in a variety of ways. In the HB (OT) book of Exodus, the author extols the importance of Moses by stating that he and God entered the tent of meeting and spoke to each other face-to-face, as friends do. Today, friends still speak face to face when they can, but most stay in contact with each other through talking on the telephone and/or texting and/or e-mail. Some friends write cards or letters and send them through the mail to each other. As everyone knows, without some form of communication, friendships die.

Meditation/Journal: Who is your best friend? How do you stay in contact with him or her?

Psalm Response: "My head is high, GOD, held high; / I'm looking to you, GOD . . . . / I've thrown in my lot with you . . . . / Show me how your work, GOD; / School me in your ways . . . . / God-friendship is for God-worshipers; / They are the ones he confides in. / If I keep my eyes on GOD, / I won't trip over my own feet." (Ps 25:1, 3a, 4, 14–15, TM)

Flower

JD: While Denver sings about flowers in a generic, collective sense, in "The Mountain Song" on the *AUTO* album, he mentions the quiet slumber of a field of columbine. He names lilacs in "Polka Dots and Moonbeams" on the *SP* album and the rose's fragrance in "Children of the Universe" on the *SH* album. In "Season Suite: Spring" on the *RMH* album, he urges his listeners to smell the flowers' sweet perfume; on the same album in "Darcy Farrow," the maiden after whom the song is named is declared to be the sweetest flower that ever bloomed over the range. He urges people to seek the graceful way of flowers in the wind, because they are his sisters and brothers in "Rhymes and Reasons" on the album with the same name. In "American Child" on the *AUTO* album, a song that expresses the freedom felt by those who live in Alaska, Denver sings about the promise made to the flowers concerning the call of the wild. On the *SDD* album, in "Wild Flowers in a Mason Jar (The Farm)," a ballad, Denver narrates a story about a grandfather who is suddenly awakened on a bus trip and who shares his dream or memory about wild flowers in a mason jar that warms him. In "Amazon (Let This Be a Voice)" on the *DD* album, Denver philosophizes about a flower blooming in the desert and how that one blossom is all flowers, and all flowers are that one blossom. He identifies it as the flower of faith. He wants the song to be a voice for the flowers.

On the *AEJD* album in "Today," he begins the song by noting that blossoms still cling to the vine. Similarly, in "No One" on the *FJ* album, he notes that parks are green and full of flowers. In "High Wind Blowin'" on the *FJ* album, he sings about his baby (beloved) who started growing flowers where nothing had ever grown. In "The Wings That Fly Us Home" on the *SP* album, he says that he dreamed that his beloved knelt and touched him with a flower. Metaphorically, the river of love has gone muddy in "River of Love" on the *FA* album, and the flowers are dying on the shore.

Scripture: ". . . I began . . . to speak words in the presence of the Most High. I said, 'O sovereign Lord, from every forest of the earth and from all its trees you have chosen one vine, and from all the lands of the world you have chosen for yourself one region, and from all the flowers of the world you have chosen for yourself one lily . . . .'" (2 Esd 5:22–24, NRSV)

Reflection: In the OT (A) book of Second Esdras, the author presents a poem about Israel's status as God's chosen people. The images were familiar to the people who read his book. Our interest here is God's choice of one lily from all the flowers of the world. The lily is one of the most mentioned of flowers in biblical literature because it represents transience and restoration. It serves as a sign of innocence, purity, and beauty. This is why the author of the OT (A) book of Second Esdras names it the flower from all flowers chosen to be God's own.

Meditation/Journal: What is your favorite flower? What does it represent?

Psalm Response: "[GOD] knows us inside and out, / keeps in mind that we're made of mud. / Men and women don't live very long; / like wildflowers they spring up and blossom, / But a storm snuffs them out just as quickly, / leaving nothing to show they were here. / GOD's love, though, is ever and always, / eternally present to all who fear him." (Ps 103:14–17, TM)

Flying

JD: Denver had a fascination with flying. In "The Eagle and the Hawk" on the *AER* album, he expresses the feeling as freedom. In "Looking for Space" on the *WIND* album, he is more specific, singing about sometimes flying like an eagle. In "Earth Day Every Day (Celebrate)" on the *ES* album, he sings about the freedom that flies at the call of the wind. In "Eli's Song" on the *SP* album, he tells Eli to give him the sign when she wants to be free; then, he tells her to see the airplane fly. The flying sparrow finds freedom in "The Flower that Shattered the Stone" on the *ES* album. He sings about slipping the surly bonds of earth, flying his plane through the halls of air, and the fact that the higher he flies the farther he goes in "Flight (The Higher We Fly)" on the *IAT* album. In "Alaska and Me" on the *HG* album, he remembers when he was a child dreaming about flying over mountains and glaciers; he also narrates the first time he flew with his father.

In "On the Wings of a Dream" on the *IAT* album, he sings about having a dream about dying and flying and flying on the wings of a dream to the place where the spirit would find him. Similarly, in "The Wings that Fly Us Home" on the *SP* album, he declares that spirit satisfied the soul's yearning and provides the wings that fly people home. On the *WIND* album in "Fly Away," he sings about a woman who is getting ready to leave him; the metaphor he uses is fly away. She's getting ready to fly away. In "Flying for Me" on the *OW* album, Denver sings about the astronauts who died in the Challenger tragedy. Denver had prepared to be on that rocket, but for some reason he could not make it. That is why he sings about the astronauts flying for him. He wanted to fly; he wanted to ride on the fiery arrow of the spaceship into the heavens. They were flying for everyone, as people on earth placed their hope in them. Denver himself died in 1997 when his light homebuilt aircraft crashed into Monterey Bay off the coast of California. In "Eagles & Horses" on *FTSS* album, he states that his soul (spirit) is a free flying thing.

Scripture: "Arise, shine; for your light has come, / and the glory of the LORD has risen upon you. / . . . [T]he LORD will arise upon you, / and his glory will appear over you. / Lift up your eyes and look around; / they all gather together, they come to you . . . . / Who are these that fly like a cloud, / and like doves to their windows? / For the coastlands shall wait for me, . . . / to bring your children from far away . . . ." (Isa 60:1, 2a, 4a, 8–9ab, NRSV)

Reflection: The freedom that Denver feels when flying is expressed by the prophet Isaiah in his description of the return of the Jewish exiles in Babylon to Jerusalem. The LORD glorifies himself by the glory with which he crowns Jerusalem. Abundance will flow again into the holy city. The former inhabitants, scattered over the face of the earth, will come home. From the west, flying like doves to the dovecotes, are the ships bringing both people and goods to the city. This vision of God's intentions for Jerusalem instills a feeling of freedom and hope for the future in the Jewish exiles, much like flying a plane filled Denver with freedom and hope.

Meditation/Journal: Remember your first airplane flight for a few seconds. How did you feel as the wings lifted you off the ground? To what can you compare that feeling in your spirituality?

Psalm Response: "Open your ears, God, to my prayer . . . . / 'Who will give me wings,' I ask— / 'wings like a dove?' / Get me out of here on dove wings; / I want some peace and quiet. / I want a walk in the country, / I want a cabin in the woods. / I'm desperate for a change / from rage and stormy weather." (Ps 55:1a, 6–8, TM)

Forest

JD: For Denver, the forest is a place of peace that needs a voice to protect it from clear cutting. Thus, he gives a voice to the forest in "Wild Montana Skies" on the *IAT* album and in "Amazon" on the *DD* album. The forest represents unity. A tree standing in a forest is all forests, and all trees are that one, he sings in Amazon" on the *DD* album. Thus, he sings about being deep in a forest in the "Foxfire Suite" on the *DD* album. On the *ES* album in "To the Wild Country," he hears the state of Alaska calling him to the forest, where he will find peace. In "Annie's Song" on the *BHA* album, he sings about how his senses are filled like a night in a forest. And in "Somethin' About" on the *IAT* album, he reflects that there is something about a forest in the late days of August. Finally, in "Boy from the Country" on the *AEJD* album, he states that the boy from the country doesn't want to see the forest for the trees. In other words, he is focused on individual trees rather than on the unity that the trees form together as a forest.

Scripture: "Sing, O heavens, for the LORD has done it; / shout, O depths of the earth; / break forth into singing, O mountains, / O forest, and every tree in it! / For the LORD has redeemed Jacob, / and will be glorified in Israel. / Thus says the LORD, your Redeemer, / who formed you in the womb: / I am the LORD, who made all things, / who alone stretched out the heavens, / who by myself spread out the earth . . . ." (Isa 44:23–24, NRSV)

Reflection: In chapter 44 of Isaiah, the prophet proclaims to the Jewish exiles in Babylon that the city of Jerusalem will be rebuilt. Then, he calls upon the heavens, the earth, the mountains, and the forest with every tree in it to rejoice at this good news. The LORD will be glorified once again in the promised land. This hymn is a call to action from one extreme—the heavens—to another extreme—the depths of the earth. The forest and every tree in it no longer can fear that the wood will be used to make idols. God is redeeming his chosen people and protecting the forest from those who would misuse it. Like Isaiah before him, Denver is a voice for the forest, which represents peace and unity, when others desire to turn it into economic gain.

Meditation/Journal: What does a forest represent for you? When you walk on a trail or drive through a forest, what do you hear?

Psalm Response: "Sing GOD a brand-new song! / Earth and everyone in it, sing! / Sing to GOD—*worship* GOD! / GOD made the heavens— / Royal splendor radiates from him, / A powerful beauty sets him apart. / Bravo, GOD, Bravo! / Everyone join in the great shout: Encore! / In awe before the beauty, in awe before the might. / Let Wilderness turn cartwheels, / Animals, come dance, / Put every tree of the forest in the choir . . . ." (Ps 96:1–2, 5–7, 12, TM)

G

Garden

JD: In a garden Denver experiences freedom, as he expresses it in "Garden Song" on the *JD* album. The song sketches the process of making a garden grow on a piece of fertile earth. After planting seeds in the earth, the warm sun and rain causes them to grow; a rake and a hoe are needed to remove weeds and small stones from the soil. The sprouting seedlings are found in long, straight rows. In "Polka Dots and Moonbeams" on the *SP* album, Denver narrates a ballad about a country dance being held in a garden, where he met a dancing partner, whom he married. While the word *garden* is not used in "Cool an' Green an' Shady" on the *BHA* album, the image the song presents is that of a garden: a grassy area, where one can lie on mother earth, close one's eyes, and loose one's self while his or her free spirit soars among dandelions, twisting vines, clover, Aspen trees, and bees—a place that is cool and green and shady.

Scripture: ". . . [T]he LORD God planted a garden . . . ; and there he put the man whom he had formed [from the dust of the ground and breathed into his nostrils the breath of life]. Out of the ground the LORD God made to grow every tree that is pleasant to the sight and good for food . . . . A river flows . . . to water the garden . . . . The LORD God took the man and put him in the garden . . . to till it and keep it." (Gen 2:8–10, 15, NRSV)

Reflection: In the second account of creation, from which the above passage comes, in the HB (OT) book of Genesis, the LORD God plants a garden for the adam (man) he has created from adamah (earth) to indicate that humans and soil are connected. This is a garden of delight named Eden. God's garden features trees with fruit and a river that provides water for the trees. This is not a garden of luxury, but it is a place for human work; the man is commissioned to till its soil and to protect it. Later, in biblical understanding, the earth is named Mother, and God is named Father. Rain falling from the Father above makes Mother earth fruitful. Of course, as Denver sings, the garden needs love and care.

Meditation/Journal: If you plant and care for either a vegetable garden or flower garden, what emotions does it illicit from you? If you do not plant nor care for a garden, what does seeing one or walking through one stir in your memories?

Canticle Response: "Wake up, North Wind, / get moving, South Wind! / Breathe on my garden, / fill the air with spice fragrance. / Oh, let my lover enter his garden! / Yes, let him eat the fine, ripe fruits. / I went to my garden, dear friend, best lover! / breathed the sweety fragrance. / I ate the fruit and honey, / I drank the nectar and wine. / Celebrate with me, friends! / Raise your glasses—'To life! To love!'" (Song 4:16ab—5:1, TM)

God

JD: God appears in many Denver songs either named or alluded. In "Thank God I'm a Country Boy" on the *BHA* album, not only does Denver identify the deity in the title of the song, but he thanks God for making him a country boy. In "No One" on the *FJ* album, he swears to God that the divinity brings him down. In "The One World," he states that the one world in which people live is one only God could design. He sings about touching the face of God in "Flight" on the *IAT* album, and in the twenty-seven-year-old man in "Rocky Mountain High" on the album with the same name one can talk to God and listen to the casual reply when camping in the mountains. In "Berkeley Woman" on the *JD* album, he declares that a woman is the sweetest fruit God ever put on a vine. His most explicit reference to the second biblical story of creation, in which God is presented as a potter, is found in "Potter's Wheel" on the *DD* album. He urges his listeners to take clay, put it on a potter's wheel, and get a little hint how God must feel. He also tells them to give the wheel a turn, to listen to it spin, and make it into the shape one wants it to be, just like God does. He summarizes the process by singing about earth, water, and wind conspiring with human hands, love, and fire to create an object on a potter's wheel.

In his songs, Denver also refers to God as Father. In "Joseph & Joe" on the *JD* album, he states that the Father is with all. He is in the hands of his Father in "On the Wings of an Eagle" on the *FJ* album. The wind is the sign of the father above in "The Flower That Shattered the Stone" on the *ES* album. In "Opposite Tables" on the *SH* album, he prays that the Father will hear him.

In "Late Nite Radio" on the *WIND* album, he declares that the Lord is still his shepherd, a reference to the first line of the HB (OT) Psalm 23. In "Two Shots," also on the *WIND* album, he states that if the good Lord had meant for the hunters to shoot ducks, he would have sent more their way. The Lord knows when the cold wind blows that it will turn one's head around in "Fire and Rain" on the *PPP* album. In "It's a Sin to Tell a Lie" on the *FJ* album, he asks the Lord to have mercy on a no-account sinner.

He acknowledges sweet Jesus Christ in "No One" on the *FJ* album, adding that it hurts to be alone. In "Fire and Rain" on the PPP album, he asks Jesus to look down upon him, to help him make a stand, and to see him through another day.

In "On the Wings of a Dream" on the *IAT* album, Denver sings about death and how our bodies leave us, but there is one who receives us: God. In "The Mountain Song" on the *AUTO* album, he echoes biblical creation stories, singing about mountain climbing with the one who made it all: God. But Denver's best presentation of God is found in "Raven's Child" on the *ES* album. He refers to God as the true king, who sits on a heavenly throne, which is never away, nor above, nor apart. He lives in the love that lives in people's hearts, sings Denver, where people find wisdom, mercy, and compassion.

Scripture: "In the day that the LORD God made the earth and the heavens, . . . the LORD God formed man from the dust of the ground, and breathed into his nostrils the breath of life, and the man became a living being. Out of the ground the LORD God made to grow every tree that is pleasant to the sight and good for food . . . ." (Gen 2:4b, 7, 9, NRSV)

Reflection: The above verses are taken from the second story of creation found in the HB (OT) book of Genesis (2:4–25). The author presents God as a potter forming man (adam) from earth (adamah), then inspiriting him with breath; the Hebrew word *ruah* can be translated as breath, spirit, or wind. The man, as his name implies, has a special relationship with the soil. After reflecting on the fact that after human beings die their bodies—for the most part—return to dust, the author of this section of Genesis concluded that their spirit lives on. In HB (OT) cosmology, their bodies are buried in the lowest level of the universe—named Sheol—while their spirits leave the middle level—named earth—and fly to the upper level—named the heavens—where God lives. This understanding is what inspired Denver to sing about touching the face of God and the one who receives us after we die; he is the one who created all things.

Meditation/Journal: What is your favorite story of creation either biblically or scientifically? Explain God's role in it. Explain the human role in it.

Psalm Response: "GOD, my God, how great you are! / beautifully, gloriously robed, / Dressed up in sunshine, / and all heaven stretched out for your tent. You set earth on a firm foundation / so that nothing can shake it, ever. / Oh yes, God brings grain from the land, / wine to make people happy, / Their faces glowing with health, / a people well-fed and hearty. / What a wildly wonderful world, GOD! / You made it all, with Wisdom at your side, / made earth overflow with your wonderful creations. / If you turned your back, / they'd die in a minute— / Take back your Spirit and they die, / revert to original mud; / Send out your Spirit and they spring to life— / the whole countryside in bloom and blossom." (Ps 104:1b–2, 5, 14–15, 24, 29–30, TM)

Grace

JD: While Denver uses the word *grace* infrequently in his songs, nevertheless, it can be said that in general Denver's songs are grace. Grace references elegance, beauty, and smoothness in form; it is pleasing and admirable. In theological understanding, grace is the action of God sharing himself with people. That is why the twenty-seven-year-old in "Rocky Mountain High" on the album with the same name seeks grace in every step he takes hiking in the mountains. In "The Ballad of St. Anne's Reel" on the *AUTO* album, the man stranded on Prince Edward Island has a clumsy body, but when he dances, he does so gracefully as a child. Without using the word grace in

"The Wings that Fly Us Home" on the *SP* album, Denver dreams the one he loves is a prophet, he dreams that he was a mountain in the wind, he dreams that his lover knelt and touched him with a flower—all are moments of grace which fill the human yearning and which live within each part and in the whole. According to Denver, grace is the fire and the wings that fly people home. Thus, in "Spirit" on the *WIND* album, he urges listeners to live with grace. He asks the precious, earth-made child in "Ancient Rhymes" on *FTSS* album to teach all how to share grace. Also, it is why Denver sings about being one with the wind and eagles and given wings to sail in gracefulness in "On the Wings of An Eagle" on the *FJ* album.

Scripture: ". . . [T]he free gift is not like the trespass [of Adam]. For if the many died through the one man's trespass, much more surely have the grace of God and the free gift in the grace of the one man, Jesus Christ, abounded for the many. And the free gift is not like the effect of the one man's sin. For the judgment following one trespass brought condemnation, but the free gift following many trespasses brings justification. If, because of the one man's trespass, death exercised dominion through that one, much more surely will those who receive the abundance of grace and the free gift of righteousness exercise dominion in life through the one man, Jesus Christ." (Rom 5:15–17, NRSV)

Reflection: In the CB (NT) Paul is the apostle of grace. Both his genuine letters and the second-generation letters written in his name by his followers drip with grace. In the passage above, grace is the action of God sharing himself with people. Jesus, God's son, is the incarnation of grace. Just like the first man's (Adam's) trespass brough death into the world, the next man's (Jesus') grace brought righteousness. In other words, through Jesus, God declared people to be in a good and healthy relationship with him. Thus, where death once reigned, grace now reigns, as demonstrated by God's act of raising Jesus from the dead. Like grace is for Denver, it is freedom to live in relationship with God for Paul. Grace cannot be earned by works; if such self-salvation were possible, then grace would no longer be grace (Rom 11:6). All people have to do is to accept God's offer of grace and cooperate with him.

Meditation/Journal: Where do you experience grace? How do you experience grace?

Psalm Response: "My heart bursts its banks, / spilling beauty and goodness. / I pour it out in a poem to the king, / shaping the river into words: / 'You're the handsomest of men; / every word from your lips is sheer grace, / and God has blessed you, blessed you so much. / Strap your sword to your side, warrior! / Accept praise! Accept due honor! / Ride majestically! Ride triumphantly! / Ride on the side of truth! / Ride for the righteous meek! Your throne is God's throne, / ever and always . . . .'" (Ps 45:1–4a, 6a, TM)

H

Heart

JD: For Denver, the word *heart* is a metaphor for emotionality, for feelings of being lonely, breaking, alive, freedom, peace, and love. In "Late Nite Radio' on the *WIND* album, Denver sings about the lonely hearts in Arkansas. On the *OW* album in "Hey There, Mr. Lonely Heart," he sings about both a lonely and a cold heart. In "The Flower That Shattered the Stone" on the *ES* album, he compares the innocent hearts of children to those who once had a heart but have been corrupted by greed and silence. In "Raven's Child" on the *ES* album, he echoes lyrics from "The Flower That Shattered the Stone," singing again about greed that has corrupted what once was a heart, how greed makes a stone of what once was a heart, and how greed has made silent what once was a heart. He acknowledges that there are hearts that long to be opened. He ends by singing that the true King—God—lives in the love that lives in people's hearts.

He states that his heart feels like breaking in "Like a Sad Song" on the *SP* album, and that even the strongest heart can be broken in "Two Different Directions" on the *DD* album. In "Seasons of the Heart" on the album with the same name, he thinks his heart is broken because he feels an emptiness inside, whereas in "The Harder They Fall" on the *DE* album, he sings that a breaking heart makes a terrible sound. A poor heart must break, he sings in "A Wild Heart Looking for Home," also on the *DE* album. The metaphor of being alive is found in "Shanghai Breezes" on the *GH3* album; in that song he sings about the one he loves being in his heart and living there. The same idea is expressed in "San Antonio Rose" on the *SP* album. A fire in the heart and an aching in the heart are found in "Wild Montana Skies" on the IAT album and in "The Gold and Beyond" on the *GH3* album.

In "It's a Sin to Tell a Lie" on the *FJ* album, he sings that it is a sin to say "I love you" if one doesn't mean it; millions of hearts have been broken that way. He tells his beloved that if she breaks his heart, he'll die, then, he crosses his heart and hopes to die! In "Relatively Speaking" on the *SH* album, he sings that sinners need the pure of heart. He declares that his heart is broken in "Seasons of the Heart" on the album with the same name. However, when it comes to seasons of the heart, he states that he cannot believe his heart when it reminds him that his beloved is not with him.

In "Easy, on Easy Street" on the *SDD* album, he asks his listeners what's on their hearts? In "To the Wild Country" on the *ES* album, he sings about his heart turning to Alaska, where he experiences freedom, which he sings about in "Hold on Tightly" on the *IAT* album. In "Flying for Me" on the *OW* album, he uses the example of the astronauts on a space shuttle, singing that they give voice to all hearts. In "Hold on Tightly" on the *IAT* album, in the heart a person can find peace and answers to questions, as is the case in "Polka Dots and Moonbeams" on the *SP* album.

However, the most used metaphor represented by the word *heart* is love. When the heart no longer flutters, one has fallen out of love in "Falling Out of Love" on the *IAT* album. In his heart, love is an illusion sings Denver in "In My Heart" on the *AUTO* album; it is how he feels in his heart, even though he knows he will have to open his heart again in "Autograph" on the same album. In "Heart to Heart" on the *SH* album, he characterizes love as another's heart to his and his heart to another; love shines heart to heart. In "Dreamland Express" on the album with the same name, he sings about seeing the very heart of the one he loves. Also, on the *DE* album in "Got My Heart Set on You," he has his heart set on another, declaring that she is everything he ever wanted. He cannot believe the feelings he has in his little heart in "I Can't Escape" on the *OW* album; his heart is open and tender to touch. In "A Country Girl in Paris" on the *HG* album he presents a contradiction; a country girl in Paris, the city of love, has a heart filled with pain, while she dreams about Nashville, Tennessee, while walking in the rain.

Scripture: One of the scribes asked Jesus, "'Which commandment is the first of all?' Jesus answered, 'The first is, "Hear, O Israel, the Lord our God, the Lord is one; you shall love the Lord your God with all your heart, and with all your soul, and with all your mind, and with all your strength." The second is this, "You shall love your neighbor as yourself." There is no other commandment greater than these.'" (Mark 12:28b–31, NRSV)

Reflection: Whereas Denver uses the word *heart* to indicate emotionality, in biblical literature heart represents the totality of one's self; it is where decisions are made. In the passage above, the Markan Jesus answers the scribe's question about the greatest commandment by quoting the HB (OT) book of Deuteronomy (6:4–9). The greatest or first commandment is self-sacrificial love of God with the totality of one's heart, soul, mind, and strength. Known as the Shema in Judaism, that is the most important commandment. The

Markan Jesus adds a second commandment from the HB (OT) book of Leviticus (19:18b) about loving one's neighbor sacrificially in the same way that one loves one's self. The Markan Jesus considers these two obligations to be one. Thus, love of God totally is connected to love of others totally, and both are connected to the love of self totally. Denver would sing about loving God, others, and self from the heart.

Meditation/Journal: What do you understand the heart to represent? Explain.

Psalm Response: "I am thanking you, GOD, from a full heart, / I'm writing the book on your wonders. / I'm whistling, laughing, and jumping for joy; / I'm singing your song, High God. / You took over and set everything right; / when I needed you, you were there, taking charge." (Ps 9:1–2, 4, TM)

Home

JD: Home is one of Denver's most used words; there is hardly any album without a song using the word *home*. In addition to home, he also uses the word *cabin* in "Wrangle Mountain Song" on the *SP* album, and the word *cottage* in "Polka Dots and Moonbeams" also on the *SP* album. Home is a place where a person lives, as Denver sings in "Back Home Again" on the album by the same name. After ten days on the road, a fire, supper, light, and a bed means that it is good to be back home again. The farm, sings Denver, feels like a long-lost friend, because the little things make a house a home. In "Wrangle Mountain Song" on the *SP* album, Denver sings about doing everything to get home because he cannot wait to get back home to the person he loves. A similar sentiment is expressed in "Shanghai Breezes" on the GH3 album; lovers long for home. In "Sweet Melinda" on the *JD* album, he is coming home at dawn. After being on the road for sixty-one days in "Southwind" on the *JD* album, he states that he could not wait until he got back home, because it is good to be home. In "On the Wings of an Eagle" on the *FJ* album, Denver, who has been away for a long time, identifies his Rocky Mountain home; his home is in the mountains. The earth has brought him home in "Healing Time on Earth," an unrecorded song.

Home is a place of safety, as Denver sings in "Hold on to Me" on the *DD* album; after being lost at sea, all were alive on arrival. He sings about finding his way back home in "Love is the Master" on the *OW* album and in "It's a Possibility" on the same album. Sometimes it is just time to go home, as stated in "American Child" on the *AUTO* album, and "On the Road" on the *BHA* album. At other times, the memory of love will bring one home, as it does in "Perhaps Love" on the *GH3* album. In "Matthew" on the *BHA* album, Denver sings about the man losing his home; in "Boy from the Country" on the *SDD* album, the boy left home when he was young; in "Wild Montana Skies" on the *IAT* album, he asks the state of Montana to give the child a home; after leaving home and maturing, the man finds his way back home. In "Rocky Mountain High" on the album with the same name, the twenty-seven-year-old man comes home to a place he had never been before! Denver sings about being surprised to find the one he loves at home in "Thought of You" on the *IAT* album, because he is a wild heart looking for a home in "A Wild Heart Looking for Home" on the *DE* album. As he sings in "Seasons of the Heart" on the album with the same name, there are times when he feels like his beloved is a stranger in his home. In "Hitchhiker" on the *SP* album, Denver sings in the person of an old hitchhiker, whom some people say will build a home in a small town and settle down, but the old man knows that he never will do that.

Finally, in "The Flower That Shattered the Stone" on the *ES* album, he sings that pure love is like a bright star in the heavens lighting the way home. Thus, home here means heaven or God.

Scripture: "Then I [, John,] saw a new heaven and a new earth . . . . And I saw the holy city, the new Jerusalem coming down out of heaven from God, prepared as a bride adorned for her husband. And I heard a loud voice from the throne saying, 'See, the home of God is among mortals. / He will dwell with them; / they will be his peoples, / and God himself will be with them. . . .'"(Rev:21:1–3, NRSV)

Reflection: The author of the CB (NT) book of Revelation presents a new creation near the end of his book. His vision is of a new heaven and a new earth. In his three-storied universe, he sees a new holy city (Jerusalem) descending from the heavens to the earth. God has descended from the top level of the universe to create a home on the middle level, where he will live with people. The desire for God and people to be united, like a man and woman in marriage, is fulfilled by God. The desire for God to be at home with people is like Denver's images for home in his songs.

Meditation/Journal: What does the word *home* mean for you? What do you consider to be the specific characteristics of your home?

Psalm Response: "What a beautiful home, GOD-of-the-Angel-Armies! / I've always longed to live in a place like this, / Always dreamed of a room in your house, / where I could sing for joy to God-alive! / Birds find nooks and crannies in your house, / sparrows and swallows make nests there. / They lay their eggs and raise their young, / singing their songs in the place where we worship. / GOD-of-the-Angel-Armies! King! God! / How blessed they are to live and sing there!" (Ps 84:1–4, TM)

I

Injustice

JD: Denver uses the word *injustice* in "It's a Possibility" on the *OW* album. He sings about fighting for more than survival and working for more than peace to make sure that all injustice will cease. Injustice is the unfair or unjust treatment of somebody or something. Injustice can be caused by the games people play, the politics of hunger, need, power, and greed. According to Denver, people fight for survival, peace, unity, and healed hearts. It is a possibility for everyone to fit into the world. In "Let Us Begin" on the *OW* album, he names injustices as weapons, the war machine, hunger, the poor, guns, power, and lives lost. In "American Child" on the *AUTO* album, he names the ability to live in freedom as an injustice for some people. Tearing down the mountains and leaving scars on the land are injustices to the earth in "Rocky Mountain High" on the album with the same name. In "Paradise" on the *RMH* album he sings about a coal train hauling Paradise away. War is the injustice in "You Say that the Battle is Over" on the *AUTO* album. Using less and doing more is the topic of "World Game" on the *IAT* album, and crack, arms sales, oil spills, and freedom are named injustices in "Raven's Child" on the *ES* album. This list of injustices in Denver songs is not exhaustive; however, it gives an indication of what Denver understood injustice to be.

Scripture: God said, "Look, you serve your own interest on your fast day, / and oppress all your workers. / Look, you fast only to quarrel and to fight and to strike with a wicked fist. / Such fasting as you do today / will not make your voice heard on high. / Is such the fast that I choose, / a day to humble oneself? / Is it to bow down the head like a bulrush, / and to lie in sackcloth and ashes? / Will you call this a fast, / a day acceptable to the LORD? / Is not this the fast that I choose: / to loose the bonds of injustice, / to undo the thongs of the yoke, / to let the oppressed go free, / and to break every yoke? / Is it not to share your bread with the hungry, / and bring the homeless poor into your house; / when you see the naked, to cover them, / and to hide yourself from your own kin? / Then your light shall break forth like the dawn, / and your healing shall spring up quickly; / your vindicator shall go before you, / the glory of the LORD shall be your rear guard." (Isa 58:3b–8, NRSV)

Reflection: The injustices named by Denver in the late twentieth century were named by the third prophet Isaiah in early fifth century BCE. In the above passage, Isaiah denounces injustice within the Jewish community. The people in Babylonian captivity want to draw near to God through fasting, but, as Isaiah records, God knows they are not interested in him. They oppress their workers; they quarrel and fight. God sees their injustice; he prefers a fast that results in the loosing of the bonds of injustice, the removal of the yoke. In other words, for God a fast sets free the oppressed; a fast permits people to share their food with the hungry, shelter the homeless, clothe the naked, and not hide from the needy in their own families. According to Isaiah, those righting of injustices is like the first light of a new day breaking over the horizon. When God sees that kind of fasting, he will rescue his people. Denver's sense of injustice is very much like that of the prophet Isaiah.

Meditation/Journal: If you fast from time to time, what is your motivation? If you do not fast, what reasons can you give for doing so. How is your fasting or lack thereof about injustices?

Psalm Response: "Open up before GOD, keep nothing back; / he'll do whatever needs to be done: / He'll validate your life in the clear light of day / and stamp you with approval at high noon. / Quiet down before GOD, / be prayerful before him. / Don't bother with those who climb the ladder, / who elbow their way to the top. / Bridle you anger, trash your wrath, / cool your pipes—it only makes things worse. / Before long the crooks will be bankrupt / GOD-investors will soon own the store. / Before you know it, the wicked will have had it; / you'll stare at his once famous place and—nothing! / Down-to-earth people will move in and take over, / relishing a huge bonanza." (Ps 37:5–11, TM)

J

Journey

JD: In "On the Road" on the *BHA* album, Denver sings about it being 1958 and not knowing who he was or what he did, while driving on a gravel road from Canada to Montana. In "Love is the Master" on the *OW* album, he sings about being on a journey to find himself. A journey can be literal, such as being in the San Juan Mountains in Colorado, or it can be figurative, a daily beginning over and over again—embracing change, getting a new telephone number, playing a new game. In "Looking for Space" on the *WIND* album, Denver sings about trying to find his own way and looking for space to find out who he is. He states that he finds himself in the sunshine and his dreams. The theme of finding self can be further explored in the entries find self and road.

Scripture: ". . . [T]he word of the LORD came to [Elijah], saying, 'What are you doing here [on Mount Horeb], Elijah?' He answered, 'I have been very zealous for the LORD, the God of hosts; for the Israelites have forsaken your covenant, thrown down your altars, and killed your prophets with the sword. I alone am left, and they are seeking my life, to take it away.' Then the LORD said to him, 'Go, return on your way to the wilderness of Damascus; when you arrive, you shall anoint Hazael as king over Aram. Also you shall anoint Jehu son of Nimshi as king over Israel, and you shall anoint Elisha son of Shaphat of Abel-meholah as prophet in your place'" (1 Kgs 19:9b–10, 15–16, NRSV)

Reflection: By the time the prophet Elijah gets to Mount Horeb (Sinai), he has been on a journey for forty days and nights—a long time. Characterized by the author of the HB (OT) book of First Kings as a Moses-like person, Elijah flees Jezreel to save his life from King Ahab and Queen Jezebel. Then, in order to find himself and the God he represents, he journeys to Horeb (Sinai), like Moses, to consult the LORD, who gives him the next steps he must take in his journey of self-discovery. Ultimately, Elijah's journey ends when he ascends in a whirlwind into heaven (2 Kgs 2:11).

Meditation/Journal: Where has your journey to find yourself taken you? What did you discover?

Psalm Response: "You're blessed when you stay on course, / walking steadily on the road revealed by GOD. / You're blessed when you follow his directions, / doing your best to find him. / that's right—you don't go off on your own; / you walk straight along the road he set. / You, GOD, prescribed the right way to live; / now you expect us to live it." (Ps 119:1–4, TM)

K

Key

JD: Denver uses the word *key* in "Rocky Mountain High" on the album with the same name. The word becomes a metaphor in the song about the twenty-seven-year-old's spiritual experience of discovering change while hiking in the Colorado Rocky Mountains. Denver characterizes the spiritual experience as a high, like that experienced by a group of people gathered around a campfire in the dark of night. According to the song (hymn?), the spiritual experience leads the hiker to walk alone in the quiet of the forest, where he discovers grace, God sharing himself with people; in the song, Denver sings about listening to God's casual reply. The spiritual experience leads the hiker to meditate on a clear blue mountain lake that is disturbed only by the wind or a fish leaping out of the water. A life full of wonder, while also knowing some healthy fear, leads the hiker to a spiritual high, just like lightning is like fire raining in the sky.

Scripture: Elijah "went in the strength of that food [given to him by an angel] forty days and forty nights to Horeb the mount of God. Then the word of the LORD came to him, saying, 'What are you doing here, Elijah?' He answered, 'I have been very zealous for the LORD, the God of hosts . . . . I alone am left . . . . He said, 'Go out and stand on the mountain before the LORD, for the LORD is about to pass by.' Now there was a great wind, so strong that it was splitting mountains and breaking rocks in pieces before the LORD, but the LORD was not in the wind; and after the wind an earthquake, but the LORD was not in the earthquake; and after the earthquake a fire, but the LORD was not in the fire; and after the fire a sound of sheer silence." (1 Kgs 19:8, 9b–12, NRSV)

Reflection: The author of the HB (OT) First Book of Kings' narrative about the prophet Elijah's experience on Mount Horeb (Sinai) is like Denver's song about the twenty-seven-year-old hiker's experience of lightning and grace in cathedral mountains. Elijah does not experience God in the same way that Moses did—lightning, a thick cloud, a blast of a trumpet, earthquake, smoke, and thunder (Exod 19:16)—but in the sound of sheer silence. TM translates the sound as "a gentle and quiet whisper" (1 Kgs 19:12). Denver classifies the sound of sheer silence or a gentle and quiet whisper as grace, a spiritual experience, a key that opens the door to the spiritual, that makes one aware of the divine presence. Like Elijah experiences God in the silence or whisper on a mountain, Denver sings about the Rocky Mountain hiker finding God in quiet solitude and pondering the serenity of the clear blue water in a mountain lake. Denver names the experience of the divine as a Rocky Mountain high; Elijah names the experience of the divine on Mount Horeb (Sinai) as the LORD. Either is a key that opens the door to the spiritual.

Meditation/Journal: Where have you experienced the presence of the divine (the LORD, God)? How do you describe it?

Psalm Response: "God is a safe place to hide, / ready to help when we need him. / We stand fearless at the cliff-edge of doom, / courageous in seastorm and earthquake, / Before the rush and roar of oceans, / the tremors that shift mountains. / Attention, all! See the marvels of GOD!" (Ps 46:1–3, 8a, TM)

L

Life

JD: According to Denver, life is the fruit of one's own creation in "Love is Everywhere" on the *WIND* album. A person is all that he or she can be, and he or she should be who he or she is, drinking life from a silver fountain like sweet water flowing to the salty sea. He urges listeners to shape their truth like a gold medallion. In "Season Suite: Summer" on the *RMH* album, Denver sings about loving the life within him; it makes him feel a part of everything he sees, and a part of everything is in him. In other words, life is the connecting thread to everyone and everything. Furthermore, he finds himself, his life, reflected in the seasons. While he rejoices in the differences between people—there is no one just like him—even as different as people are, they are still the same, because the same life animates them. That is why he can repeat his words in "Season Suite: Spring" about loving the life within himself and feeling a part of everything, while a part of everything is in him. In "Rocky Mountain High," Denver characterizes that as a life full of wonder. In "Amazon" on the *DD* album, he further explores the idea of being part of everything and everything being a part of him. A bird singing in the jungle indicates that that one song is all music, and all songs are that one; it is the song of life. And, as he sings in "The Foxfire Suite: Spring is Alive" on the *DD* album, life is good. In "All This Joy" on the *HG* album, he groups joy, sorrow, promise, and pain together and sings that such is life. Then, he adds city and world of joy, sorrow, promise, and pain and repeats that such is life. In "Song for the Life" on the *AUTO* album, Denver sings about the life he has found, a life that keeps his feet on the ground; he sings about learning to listen to the sunset or the dying-down breeze. Also, in "American Child" on the *AUTO* album, he sings about a burning inside him for the pioneer life in Alaska. Life is more than always choosing sides, he sings in "Children of the Universe" on the *SH* album; life also lives within the silent hills.

Scripture: Jesus said to the crowd, "'Take care! Be on your guard against all kinds of greed; for one's life does not consist in the abundance of possessions.' Then he told them a parable: 'The land of a rich man produced abundantly. And he thought to himself, "What should I do, for I have no place to store my crops?" Then he said, 'I will do this: I will pull down my barns and build larger ones, and there I will store all my grain and my goods. And I will say to [myself, "Self], you have ample goods laid up for many years; relax, eat, drink, be merry." But God said to him, 'You fool! This very night your life is being demanded of you. And the things you have prepared, whose will they be?'" (Luke 12:15–20, NRSV)

Reflection: The above parable is one among several in Luke's Gospel about the dangers of possessing wealth. The author of Luke's Gospel considers hoarding to be greed; life, according to the author's Jesus, does not consist of possessions, as it doesn't consist of possessions in Denver's songs. Life is what one makes it to be. In the Lukan schema, possessions are given to some by God to be given away to those who have none. Giving away possessions is life within, as contrasted to hoarding or life outside. The uniquely Lukan parable focuses on the good, inner life, the truth one lives by. Life is the fruit of every person's creation; life can be shared or given away, or life can be hoarded or stored. Both have consequences, according to Denver and the author of Luke's Gospel.

Meditation/Journal: Do you hoard life or give away life? What percentage of your life is spent saving, and what percent is spent hoarding? Is life more without you or within you? Explain.

Psalm Response: "I say to the LORD, 'You are my Lord; / I have no good apart from you.' / I bless the LORD who gives me counsel; / in the night also my heart instructs me. / I keep the LORD always before me; / because he is at my right hand, I shall not be moved. / You show me the path of life. / In your presence there is fullness of joy; / in your right hand are pleasures forevermore." (Ps 16:2, 7–8, 11, NRSV)

Light

JD: While light, energy producing brightness that makes seeing possible, is present in some Denver songs, it is not used as much as might be expected. In "African Sunrise" on the *DE* album, Denver sings about the African sunrise being the light of a brand-new day. Besides the words *sunrise* and *light* in "African Sunrise," in other songs Denver uses dawn, morning, and sun. In "Wild Montana Skies" on the *IAT* album, Denver asks that the state of Montana give the young man a light in his eyes. On the *OW* album in "Flying for Me," he sings that the Challenger astronauts were flying for him and for everyone to try to see a brighter day for each and every one; they gave their light. In "Baby, You Look Good to Me Tonight" on the *SP* album, he sings about a trucker who has to stop and eat while he still has light, while in "Southwind" on the *JD* album, he signs about the lights going down in an east Texas town. He compares pure, growing love to a bright star in heaven that lights the way home in "The Flower that Shattered the Stone" on the *ES* album. In "Dancing with the Mountains" on the *AUTO* album, he asks his listeners if they were present the night they lost the lightning and if they were present to see the famous and the lightning—flashes of light in the sky when there is a discharge of atmospheric electricity in the clouds or between the clouds and the earth usually during a thunderstorm. Thus, while there is little doubt that light is preferred to darkness, light energy that produces brightness that makes seeing possible is a metaphor for understanding both people and the world in which people live.

Scripture: "The LORD went in front of [the Israelites] in a pillar of cloud by day, to lead them along the way, and in a pillar of fire by night, to give them light, so that they might travel by day and by night. Neither the pillar of cloud by day nor the pillar of fire by night left its place in front of the people." (Exod 13:21–22, NRSV)

Reflection: In the HB (OT) book of Exodus, light from a pillar of fire enables the Israelites to travel away from Egypt toward the promised land. While it looks like there are two pillars—one of cloud and one of fire—the author of the book clarifies that they are one and the same; he states that "the LORD in the pillar of fire and cloud" (Exod 14:24, NRSV) caused a panic among the Egyptian army pursuing the Israelites. The cloud and fire are visible, biblical signs of God's presence among the Israelites. In other words, they are the energy producing brightness that makes seeing possible; they are manifestations of the divine.

Meditation/Journal: In what specific ways do you use light, either natural or artificial, throughout your day? Make a list. Then, with the list in hand, ask yourself: What do I notice about my use of light?

Psalm Response: "Listen, dear friends, to God's truth, / bend your ears to what I tell you. / He performed miracles in plain sight . . . / in Egypt, out on the fields . . . . / He split the [Red] Sea and they walked right through it; / he piled the waters to the right and the left. / He led [the Israelites] by day with a cloud, / led them all the night long with a fiery torch." (Ps 78:1, 12–14, TM)

Love

JD: There are many Denver songs that contain the word *love*. In fact, just analyzing the Denver songs using the word *love* could be the topic of a book! Philosophizing, Denver sings that love is seeing all the infinite in one in "The Wings that Fly Us Home" on the *SP* album. In "Love is the Master" on the *OW* album, he sings that love is the master of everything we do. On the same album in "True Love Takes Time," he declares that true love, which is very hard to find, takes time; it requires a heart open and tender. In "Perhaps Love" on the *SH* album, Denver compares love to a resting place, a window, an open door, a cloud, steel, a way of life, a feeling, an ocean, fire, and rain, sometime holding on, sometime letting go, and on the same album in "Seasons of the Heart," he states that love is the reason he went where he went, what he hoped to find, and his dream. After singing about getting deeper in love and feeling the other person's love in "Till You Opened My Eyes" on the *SDD* album, he sings that love is a mystery.

Even though an old guitar taught Denver to sing a long song in "This Old Guitar" on the *BHA* album, in "San Antonio Rose" on the *SP* album, he sings about his broken song of love—empty words—that lives alone in his heart. On the *IAT* album in "Falling Out of Love," he compares falling out of love to losing one's best friend. There are no words to describe the pain and fear, he sings. The heart no longer flutters. When true love ends, it is an incredible loss. However, at the end of the song, Denver sings that he doesn't think true love ever ends. Nevertheless, in "Thought of You" on the *IAT* album, he sings that it hurts much to be in love. In "Country Love" on the *SDD* album, he sings about Nashville tears being signs that point to broken hearts, lives, and families that love splits apart; he names it love gone wrong. Country love, according to Denver, consists of kisses in the kitchen; it is honest and true; and it is being home with one's family. It is the way that Denver loves. Country love also consists of silky nights and warm familiar hands. When Nashville night is the question, sings Denver, country love is the answer.

In "River of Love" on the *FA* album, he names it the river of love gone muddy. And in "Two Different Directions" on the DD album, he sings about two people who say they love each other, but they are moving in different directions, which makes their true love alone. Then, love turns to anger and hate; as long as people move in different directions, true love must wait, sings Denver. In "Relatively Speaking" on the *SH* album, Denver sings about love needing contrasts, like savage hurtful fights and lonely beds. On the *OW* album in "Love Again," Denver expresses feelings about not believing that he would ever love again, about being afraid that he might never love again, even though he was falling in love again. On the *BHA* album in "Annie's Song," he calls her to let him love her again by enjoying her laughter, dying in her arms, lying beside her, and being always with her.

When it comes to expressions of love, Denver sings about finding an answer to the mystery of what he calls love's most precious seed in "Hey There, Mr. Lonely Heart" on the *OW* album. He asks if it consists of touching, kissing, or needing to give, while acknowledging that love is strong. He states that true love is the answer; the gift is in the giving, and true love is all that people need. In "Home Grown Tomatoes" on the *HG* album, Denver identifies one thing that money cannot buy: true love. In "I Remember Romance" on the *IAT* album, he sings about love by candlelight, and in "Somethin' About" on the same album, he tells his baby that there is something about the way she loves him and the way they kiss and touch each other. In "For Baby (For Bobbie)" on the *RMH* album, he sings that he will love her more than anybody can, as he sees the reflection of love in her eyes. On the *SP* album in "Baby, You Look Good to Me Tonight," he asks the other person if she believes in love at first sight. Later, he adds that he was born to love and there is time to make love. In "Never a Doubt" on the *HG* album, he refers to the magic of love—someday one's true love will arrive. He adds that what is broken with love can be mended. The love he knew during a few days and that he remembers was a reason for living in "The Game Is Over" on the *FJ* album; and is everywhere, always safe, and true in "Heart to Heart" on the *SH* album. It is a light that shines from one person's heart to the other person's heart; the other side of lonely is falling in love, sings Denver. Exactly where love comes from is where it is going!

Where is the love all people need, he asks in "Hold on Tightly" on the *IAT* album. He adds that some people take love over gold. In "Wild Montana

Skies" on the *IAT* album, he asks Montana to give the boy born in the Bitterroot Valley the love of a good family and a wife of his own. After growing up and leaving home, the man returns, because he loves the land. In "Boy from the Country" on the *SDD* album, the boy left home when he was young after telling others that they should love the land. In "Matthew" on the *BHA* album, love is a way to live and die, whereas in "Back Home Again" on the same album, love lights the way. Love is everywhere in "Love is Everywhere" on the *WIND* album. Denver summarizes that one man can love; a bright man has a strong love in "What One Man Can Do" on the *SH* album. In "Autograph" on the album with the same name, Denver sings that part of his autograph is found in the love that he brings. He thanks God for a precious day with a heart full of love in "Falling Leaves (The Refugees)" on the *HG* album, and states that a pure love still grows in the hearts of children in "The Flower That Shattered the Stone" on the *ES* album. A good summary of Denver's multiple thoughts about love can be found in "All This Joy" on the *HG* album. He sings that all joy, sorrow, promise, and pain are aspects of love. Then, he sings that every city and the world is full of joy, sorrow, promise, and pain, and such is love.

Scripture: "Love is patient; love is kind; love is not envious or boastful or arrogant or rude. It does not insist on its own way; it is not irritable or resentful; it does not rejoice in wrongdoing, but rejoices in the truth. It bears all things, believes all things, hopes all things, endures all things. Love never ends." (1 Cor 13:4–8a, NRSV)

Reflection: In the above selection from Paul's First Letter to the Corinthians, the apostle to the Gentiles presents the way of love. The Greek word is *agape*, one of four words for love in Greek; English has but one word for love. *Agape* is self-sacrificing love. Paul uses *agape* to explain how followers of Jesus love: patiently, kindly; love is never jealous, never braggartly, never self-vaunting, and never ill-mannered. Because it is self-sacrificing, the person who lives the way of love does not insist on having his or her way, and is not irritated or resentful of the plurality of truth; in fact the person who loves self-sacrificially rejoices in truth. Not only is the person who *agapes* (loves self-sacrificially) able to bear all things, but he or she believes all things, hopes all things, and endures all things. Love never ceases, because it comes from God, who loves people the way he loves himself. Some of Denver's songs that mention love are *agapeic*; they reflect the self-sacrificial aspect of love.

Meditation/Journal: Out of your favorite Denver songs that mention love, which do you think reflect Paul's way of love? Explain.

Psalm Response: ". . . GOD's Word is solid to the core; everything he makes is sound inside and out. / He loves it when everything fits, / when his world is in plumb-line true. / Earth is drenched / in GOD's affectionate satisfaction. / Watch this: God's eye is on those who respect him, / the ones who are looking for his love. / . . . [O]ur hearts brim with joy / since we've taken for our own his holy name. / Love us, GOD, with all you've got— / that's what we're depending on." (Ps 33:4–5, 18, 21–22, TM)

M

Memory

JD: While it is true to say that Denver's songs are, in general, based on memories of experiences he had—such as love, travel, mountains, forests, oceans, flying, dreams, etc.—there are a few songs where he sings about all the memories that he received from "Matthew" on the *BHA* album, or the fact that all his memories lay in the life of the highway in "All of My Memories" on the *AER* album. In "Perhaps Love" on the *SH* album, he sings about how the memory of love will see him through and bring him home. In "True Love Takes Time" on the *OW* album, he acknowledges that there are many memories in the mystery of time that dance around in one's mind and whisper endlessly. In "San Antonio Rose" on the *SP* album, he says that in dreams he lives with a memory beneath the stars. The twenty-seven-year-old in "Rocky Mountain High" on the album with the same name, changes so fast that he loses a friend but keeps his memory. In "Islands" on the *SH* album, Denver refers to the dark sands of memory which he is leaving behind in "All of My Memories" on the *AER* album. Thus, the ability to retain information about past events and experiences and to retrieve it and set the words that describe the experience to music is what Denver did to preserve his memories.

Scripture: "Wisdom praises herself, / and tells of her glory in the midst of her people. / In the assembly of the Most High she opens her mouth, / and in the presence of his hosts she tells of her glory: / '. . . [T]he memory of me is sweeter than honey, / and the possession of me sweeter than the honeycomb. / Those who eat of me will hunger for more, / and those who drink of me will thirst for more.'" (Sir 24:1–2, 20–21, NRSV)

Reflection: All of chapter 24 of the OT (A) book of Sirach is a single poem praising wisdom; it is presented as wisdom personified. In other words, wisdom is the speaker of the poem. Because God created her before anything else, she proclaims herself to both those living on earth (her people) and those living in the heavens (the Most High God and his army). According to the author, the memory of wisdom is like the sweetness of honey in the honeycomb. Using the metaphors of eating and drinking, the author presents her stating that those who eat and drink her will hunger and thirst for more of her. In other words, those who remember her will always want more. Similarly, Denver was constantly in need of new experiences so that he could sing about his memories of those events.

Meditation/Journal: For whom is your fondest memory? Explain. For what experience is your fondest memory? Write a poem (or song) about it.

Psalm Response: "All the ends of the earth shall remember and turn to the LORD; / and all the families of the nations shall worship before him. / For dominion belongs to the LORD, / and he rules over the nations. / Posterity will serve him; / future generations will be told about the Lord, / and proclaim his deliverance to a people yet unborn, / saying that he has done it." (Ps 22:27–28, 30–31, NRSV)

Moon

JD: While Denver mentions the sun more often than he does the moon in his songs, he makes sure that his listeners know that the moon they see anywhere in the world is the same one sung about in "Shanghai Breezes" on the *GH3* album. In "Wild Flowers in a Mason Jar (The Farm)" on the *SDD* album, he mentions the moonlit land, while in "I Remember Romance" on the *IAT* album, he is found laughing at the moon, and in "Cowboy's Delight" on the *WIND* album, he talks to the moon. Likewise, in "San Antonia Rose" on the *SP* album, he sees the moon in all its splendor, and in "Eclipse" on the *BHA* album, he sings about a shaded moon on the earth hanging lazily, while the old man in the moon smiles and laughs. In "On the Road" on the *BHA* album, he records that the man in the moon told him to go home, because it was getting late and he was soon going to turn off his light. In "Love Is Everywhere" on the *WIND* album, he states that old man moon is on a snow-covered mountain. In "Ancient Rhymes" on *FTSS* album, it is two days before the full moon, in which some walk in "Children of the Universe" on the *SH* album. In "Song of Wyoming" on the *WIND* album, Denver sings about the old prairie moon rising and shining light.

On the *SP* album in "Polka Dots and Moonbeams" he sees moon-beams, just like he sees a full moon over India in "It's About Time" on the album with the same name. He watches the distant moonlight fill the coming of the tides in "Children of the Universe" on the *SH* album, and he dreams of touching his beloved's face in moonlight in "A Wild Heart Looking for Home" on the *DE* album. Captive moonlight waits for dawn in "Season Suite: Summer" on the *RMH* album. In other words, the earth's only natural satellite reflects light from the sun to the earth until the bright light of dawn overwhelms it.

Scripture: "It is the moon that marks the changing seasons, / governing the times, their everlasting sign. / From the moon comes the sign for festal days, / a light that wanes when it completes its course. / The new moon, as its name suggests, renews itself; / how marvelous it is in this change, / a beacon to the hosts on high, / shining in the vault of the heavens!" (Sir 43:6–8, NRSV)

Reflection: In Hebrew (Israelite, Jewish) cosmology, the middle level of the three-storied universe is the earth. Under a dome (sky, vault) that covers the earth moves the sun and the moon. The phases of the moon are the basis for the Jewish calendar. A new moon marks the beginning of each month. Just as the moon reflects the sun's light, the Jewish people reflect the light of God and the Torah he gave them. Just like the moon waxes and wanes, God's people have endured hardship and restoration. The moon's cycles serve as a metaphor for life, which renews itself. In Christianity, the moon plays a role in determining the date for Easter every year. It is the first Sunday after the first full moon after the Spring Equinox; this means that Easter usually falls between March 20 and April 25. While the calculation of the moon's phases do not influence people today, in Sirach's reflections, the moon remains one of God's best creations. In Denver's music, the moon sets the scene for mystical lyrics.

Meditation/Journal: What role does the moon play in your daily life? Explain.

Psalm Response: "GOD, brilliant Lord, / yours is a household name. / I look up at your macro-skies, dark and enormous, / your handmade sky-jewelry, / Moon and stars mounted in their settings. / Then I look at my micro-self and wonder, / Why do you bother with us? / Why take a second look our way? / GOD, brilliant Lord, / your name echoes around the world." (Ps 8:1, 3–4, 8, TM)

Mountains

JD: Because Denver established his home in Aspen, Colorado, he lived in the Rocky Mountains. There is hardly an album without a song that mentions mountains. There is something about mountains that rise to the heavens, Denver sings in "Somethin' About" on the *IAT* album. In "On the Wings of An Egle" on the *FJ* album, he sings about having his home in the mountains, and if he ever left, he would return again to his Rocky Mountain home. In "The Mountain Song" on the *AUTO* album, he sings a mountain song, stating that he skied on crystal pathways to a mountain peak that was very tall, and he walked the mighty summits with the one who made it all (God). He sings that when one loves a mountain lady, one sings a mountain song. In "How Mountain Girls Can Love" also on the *AUTO* album, he sings that mountain girls can love. From the perspective of a freely flowing river, it looks like the mountain rises, he sings in "The Flower that Shattered the Stone" on the *ES* album. In "All of My Memories" on the *AER* album, from the same perspective as the previous song, he sings about the mountains making love to the sky. He wishes Jesse would take him high on a mountain top in "Nothing but a Breeze" on the *SH* album. He is high on a mountain in the Smokie Mountains in "The Foxfire Suite: Spring is Alive" on the *DD* album. In "The Gold and Beyond" on the *GH3* album, his perspective is on the side of a mountain; in the eyes of the mountain all people are equal. Likewise, in "Joseph & Joe" on the *JD* album, he sings about Joe living on the side of a mountain in the mountains.

Denver sings about having been to the mountains, climbed through the sky, shouldered their whiteness, watched their gold fly, stood in their treasure, and shook at their might in "Cowboy's Delight"—a song of the mountain—on the *WIND* album. If the future of life could lie before us, Denver sings, we wouldn't need to climb a mountain, because we would know what is on the other side in "Gravel on the Ground" on the *SDD* album. Because of his experiences in the mountains, he can sing about riding a storm across the mountains in "Wild Montana Skies" on the *IAT* album; about the quiet life in the mountains in "Wrangle Mountain Song" on the *SP* album; about how he can rest in the mountains in "To the Wild Country" on the *ES* album; how Annie fills his senses like the mountains in springtime in "Annie's Song" on the *BHA* album; and how men and the mountains are brothers in "Rocky Mountain Suite" on the *FA* album. Thus, for all those reasons, he sings about raising his son Zachary in the mountains in "Zachary and Jennifer" on the *FA* album. He would rather live on the side of a mountain, he sings in "I'd Rather Be a Cowboy" on the *FA* album, than wonder through canyons of concrete and steel (city streets). He loves the mountains so much that he dances with them, and sings that when all dance with the mountains, people are one in "Dancing with the Mountains" on the *AUTO* album. He dreams that he was a mountain in the wind in "The Wings That Fly Us Home" on the *SP* album. In "Rocky Mountain High" on the album with the same name, he sings about a twenty-seven-year-old man whose life was far away when he first came to the mountains, but after climbing cathedral peaks, he found himself.

In what can be called Denver's protest mountain songs, he notes that after the twenty-seven-year-old found himself, he wondered why people try to tear down the mountains in "Rocky Mountain High" on the album with the same name. In "Eclipse" on the *ES* album, he mentions a heavy smog which prohibits him from seeing the mountains, and it is enough to make him cry. In "Rocky Mountain Suite" on the *FA* album, he stresses that life in the mountains is living in danger from too many people and too many machines. Thus, for Denver, mountains—no matter where they are located—provide a healthy life for those who live among them, and that quiet life ought to be protected.

Scripture: "On the morning of the third day [after the Israelites had arrived at Mount Sinai (Hoeb)] there was thunder and lightning, as well as a thick cloud on the mountain, and a blast of a trumpet so loud that all the people who were in the camp trembled. Moses brought the people out of the camp to meet God. They took their stand at the foot of the mountain. Now Mount Sinai was wrapped in smoke, because the LORD had descended upon it in fire; the smoke went up like the smoke of a kiln, while the whole mountain shook violently. As the blast of the trumpet grew louder and louder, Moses would speak and God would answer him in thunder. When the LORD descended upon Mount Sinai, to the top of the mountain, the LORD summoned Moses to the top of the mountain, and Moses went up." (Exod 19:16–20, NRSV)

Reflection: Ancient people's cosmology consisted of a three-level universe. On the first level below the earth is where the dead lived; on the middle, plate-like surface of the earth is where people lived; and above the dome of the sky is where God lived. A mountain connected earth and heaven; that is why ancient people thought that the gods and the LORD God lived on a mountain top. Known as a theophany, the appearance of God is described using the number three and the elements of nature. Three indicates the spiritual order; it generates an expectation; something new is about to happen—all caused by the divine presence. One natural element of a theophany is thunder; not only is it a biblical sign of the divine presence, but it is the way that God answers Moses. The thick cloud, often seen on mountain peaks, is another sign of God's presence. Lightning, a sign of divine glory, represents the unapproachable presence of the divine. The trumpet blast is used to summon the Israelites to meet their God, who descends from the top level of the universe to the middle level to meet his people. He comes in the form of fire with smoke. The violent shaking of the mountain is an earthquake, another biblical element of a theophany. Denver uses his own experiences to sing about mountains. Biblical authors used signs that their neighbors used to indicate the presence of their god(s); biblical authors portray the appearance of the LORD God using a number along with the elements of a storm: thunder, lightning, clouds, fire, and smoke.

Meditation/Journal: What things do you use to become aware of the divine presence? Make a list.

Psalm Response: "Up with God! / Sing hymns to God; / all heaven, sing out; / clear the way for the coming of Cloud-Rider. / Enjoy GOD, / cheer when you see him! / The Lord gave the word; / thousands called out the good news . . . . / On that day . . . snow fell on Black Mountain. / You huge mountains, Bashan mountains, / mighty mountains, dragon mountains. / All you mountains not chosen, / sulk now, and feel sorry for yourselves. / For this is the mountain God has chosen to live on; / he'll rule from this mountain forever." (Ps 68:1a, 4, 11, 14–16, TM)

N

Night

JD: Denver sings about night in general—a daily period of darkness, to-night—the night of a present day, darkness—the absence of light, lonely night—the feeling of being alone and sad during the night, and midnight—the midpoint of night. In "Poems, Prayers, and Promises" on the album with the same name, he states that he spent a night or two all on his own and that the nights are seldom long. In "I'm Sorry" on *WC* album he cannot sleep at night. He expresses the same sentiment in "Sticky Summer Weather" on the *TMT* album; the sticky summer weather makes the nights seem to last forever. Likewise, In "High Wind Blowin'" on the *FJ* album, he sings about not sleeping tonight because of the noise of the high wind and the cold. He is more specific in "Annie's Song" on the *BHA* album, singing that she fills up his sense like a night in a forest, which is echoed again in "Love is the Master" on the *OW* album as a night in the wilderness, and in "It's a Possibility" on the *OW* album as the heart being a beacon in the night. On the *WIND* album in "Love is Everywhere," he urges his listeners to follow their hearts like a race with the sun to the edge of night. Similarly, he dreams night into morning in "Till You Opened My Eyes" on the *SDD* album. In "On the Wings of a Dream" on the *IAT* album, he sings about his father being in his heart from the dark of the night to the dawn. In "Whiskey Basin Blues" on the *FA* album, he begins the song by setting it on a snow-covered night in Wyoming. Similarly, in "How Mountain Girls Can Love" on the *AUTO* album, he's riding at night on a cold wind in the high country. In "Whalebones and Crosses" on the same AUTO album, he sings for his father and how the night becomes the day. The night is nearly gone in "Goodbye Again" on the *RMH* album, as Denver gets ready to leave at five o'clock in the morning. In "The Cowboy and the Lady" on the *SDD* album, it is a rainy night in Nashville, Tennessee. In "Earth Day Every Daty (Celebrate)" on the *ES* album, Denver begins by calling to mind the cry of a loon on a lake in the night. His most extensive use of night is found on the *DE* album; he sings about last night in "Dreamland Express;" about one of those nights in "Got My Heart Set on You;" about a Saturday night in Aspen, Colorado, in "The Harder They Fall;" and how a night in the city can drive one crazy in "A Wild Heart Looking for a Home."

The word *tonight* is used in "Baby, You Look Good to Me Tonight" on the *SP* album; it is also used in "Claudette" on the *DE* album—he wants to see her tonight and kiss her good night. The absence of light—darkness— is used three times on the *WIND* album in "Windsong"—where the wind weaves the darkness; in "Cowboy's Delight"—where the cowboy is told to make friends with the darkness; and in "Shipmates and Cheyenne"—where Denver sings about holding onto one more rising sun until daylight and darkness are done. Similarly, in "Calypso" on the same album, he sings about the ship bringing its passengers to light up the darkness and show the way. In "River of Love" on the *FA* album, Denver sings about blue skies having turned to darkness, much like he does in "You Say that the Battle Is Over" on the *AUTO* album, singing about the darkness of life; in "Pegasus" on the *SP* album being dark with sleep and dark with sound; in "Love Is the Master" on the *OW* album being the darkest of night; and on the same album in "Love Again" being afraid of the dark.

An old guitar is a friend to have on a cold and lonely night in "This Old Guitar" on the *BHA* album. In "Fly Away" on the WIND album, Denver sings about nights having gone sad and shady, while in "On the Wings of a Dream" on the *IAT* album, he sings that the night that he is living through grows cold. On the same album in "I Remember Romance," he sings about bubble baths at night. On the *AER* album in "All of My Memories," he sings about nights in old motels sleeping alone. However, in "Thought of You" on the *IAT* album, he remembers the nights and the passionate fights and he knows that he loves someone and he always will. It's a long night sleeping alone in "Prisoners" on the *RMH* album, while the night never ends with one night stands in "Sleepin' Alone" on the *SDD* album. On the *DE* album in "Don't Close Your Eyes Tonight," not only does he ask the person to whom he is singing not to close her eyes, but he urges her to let it be him tonight. Basically, for Denver being lost in the night all alone and where nights are so dark and long are signs of having no one to love, as In "A Wild Heart Looking for a Home" on the *DE* album. When a Nashville, Tennessee, night is the question, the answer is country love, sings Denver in "Country Love" on the *SDD* album.

The half-way point through the night is midnight, as he sings between midnight and the dawn in "Late Nite Radio" on the *WIND* album. It is just plain midnight in "Whalebones and Crosses" and "American Child" on the *AUTO* album. However in "Wild Flowers in a Mason Jar (The Farm)" on the *SDD* album, there is a gorgeous midnight and a midnight highway. In "River" on the *FJ* album, when it is quiet at night, people can stare at the sky. In "Nobody Can Take My Dreams from Me" on the *FJ* album, he sings about minstrels and beggars coming out at nighttime and singing.

The word *nighttime* is rolling his way in "Song of Wyoming" on the *WIND* album, as it is filled with love in "Pegasus" on the *SP* album. On the same album in "Like a Sad Song," it is in the nighttime that he knows that it is the right time to hold the person he loves close and tell her that he loves her. Thus, Denver sings about night being a daily period of darkness; tonight being the night of a present day; darkness being the absence of light; a lonely night being the feeling of being alone and sad during the night; and midnight, the midpoint of night.

Scripture: ". . . [T]he LORD said to Moses, 'Stretch out your hand toward heaven so that there may be darkness over the land of Egypt, a darkness that can be felt.' So Moses stretched out his hand toward heaven, and there was dense darkness in all the land of Egypt for three days. People could not see one another, and for three days they could not move from where they were; but all the Israelites had light where they lived. At midnight the LORD struck down all the firstborn in the land of Egypt, from the firstborn of Pharaoh who sat on his throne to the firstborn of the prisoner who was in the dungeon, and all the firstborn of the livestock. That was for the LORD a night of vigil, to bring them out of the land of Egypt. That same night is a

vigil to be kept for the LORD by all the Israelites throughout their generations." (Exod 10:21–23; 12:29, 42, NRSV)

Reflection: The author of the HB (OT) book of Exodus uses night to focus attention on Egypt in darkness, while Israel is in light. The ninth of ten
plagues features the LORD telling Moses to call darkness from heaven upon
Egypt for three days. The reader must be aware that this directive is in oppo-
sition to the understanding that God dwelt in light. While divine darkness
descends upon Egypt, divine light shines upon Israel. The tenth plague also
occurs at night—midnight exactly! The darkness over Egypt is equated with
death, as the firstborn of people and animals die. However, the light shines
upon the Israelites, as the pharaoh permits them to leave the darkness of
their slavery and escape to the light of freedom. The Israelites are instructed
to keep a vigil on the evening before their yearly commemoration of their
escape from Egypt. In the darkness of the night, they are to remember that
they were chosen by God; they were enlightened. Thus, night is a holy time
to keep vigil for the light.

Meditation/Journal: When have you discovered yourself to be in the night,
when, upon careful reflection, you discovered that you were really in the
light?

Psalm Response: "Is there anyplace I can go to avoid your Spirit [, GOD]?
/ to be out of your sight? / If I climb to the sky, you're there! / If I go underground, you're there! / If I flew on morning's wings, / to the far western
horizon, / You'd find me in a minute— / you're already there waiting! / Then
I said to myself, 'Oh, he even sees me in the dark! / At night I'm immersed
in the light!' / It's a fact: darkness isn't dark to you; / night and day, darkness
and light, they're all the same to you." (Ps 139:7–12, TM)

O

Ocean

JD: There is something about the ocean as it rises to meet the shoreline,
sings Denver in "Somethin' About" on the *IAT* album. He adds that there is
something about a river and the way it runs to meet the sea. This fascination with the ocean and sea is also found in "I Want to Live" on the album
with the same name. The mighty blue ocean keeps rolling on every shore

in "Islands" on the *SH* album, while it becomes the deep blue sea in "Nothing but a Breeze" on the same album. While gazing at the ocean, he asks his listeners if they have ever seen the breaching of a whale or watched the dolphins frolic in the sea's foam. In "Perhaps Love" on the *GH3* album, he suggests that love may be like the ocean full of conflict and full of change. In "Calypso" on the *WIND* album, he begins singing about sailing on a dream on a crystal-clear ocean, and in "Earth Day Every Day (Celebrate)" on the *ES* album, he urges people to celebrate both land and sea. He needs his beloved like the ocean needs the land in "Relatively Speaking" on the *SH* album. Indeed, Denver does celebrate the ocean, as he sings that he is one who dances with it in "Dancing with the Mountains" on the *AUTO* album. In "Hold on Tightly" on the *IAT* album, he compares being lost in a boat on the ocean or lost in a ship at sea to one who is free. In "American Child" on the *AUTO* album, he calls the ocean an icy blue sea. On the *DD* album in "Amazon," he lets his song be a voice for the ocean. The one world in which all live consists of—among other things—the oceans in "The One World," the 1988 theme song for the Global Forum.

Scripture: ". . . Moses stretched out his hand over the sea. The LORD drove the sea back by a strong east wind all night, and turned the sea into dry land; and the waters were divided. The Israelites went into the sea on dry ground, the waters forming a wall for them on their right and on their left. The Egyptians pursued, and went into the sea after them, all of Pharaoh's horses, chariots, and chariot drivers. . . . Moses stretched out his hand over the sea, and at dawn the sea returned to its normal depth. As the Egyptians fled before it, the LORD tossed the Egyptians into the sea. The waters returned and covered the chariots and the chariot drivers, the entire army of Pharaoh that had followed them into the sea; not one of them remained." (Exod 14:21–23, 27–28, NRSV)

Reflection: The key event in the HB (OT) is the narrative of the Israelites crossing the Red Sea (Sea of Reeds). In biblical understanding, the sea or ocean represents chaos, which only God can order. And that is exactly what the LORD does through Moses. After Moses stretches his hand over the sea, God orders the chaos by splitting it into two parts, through which the Israelites escape Pharaoh's army and march to freedom. Then, after all the Israelites are across on dry ground, the LORD tells Moses to stretch his hand over the sea again. As the ocean returns to its normal depth, Pharaoh's army drowns, giving the Israelites evidence that he is with them and will protect them. The Israelites were fascinated by the parting of the Sea of Reeds, just like Denver is awed by the vastness and power of the ocean and seas.

Canticle Response: "I'm singing my heart out to GOD—what a victory! / He pitched horse and rider into the sea. / GOD is my strength, GOD is my song, / and yes! GOD is my salvation. / *This* is the kind of God I have / and I'm telling the world! / *This* is the God of my father— / I'm spreading the news far and wide! / GOD is a fighter, / pure GOD, through and through. / Pharaoh's chariots and army / he dumped in the sea. / Wild ocean waters poured over them; / they sank like a rock in the deep blue sea." (Exod 15:1b–4a, 5, TM)

P

Paradise

JD: Denver's song "Paradise" on the *RMH* album, is a lament for the destruction of natural landscapes using Muhlenberg County, Kentucky, as an example. Denver names the coal-mining town Paradise, which was destroyed by Peabody, a coal-mining company which strip-mined the land and, after all the coal was extracted, abandoned the operation. In other words, the pristine environment was transformed into a despoiled landscape. While some people considered coal mining to be progress, Denver considered it to be a tragedy. In "Like a Sad Song" on the *SP* album, Denver sings that he sometimes feels like a sad song, when he is all alone without the person he loves. He sings that Paradise was made for her and him. In "Sweet Melinda" on the *JD* album, he records seeing a sign in Texas that read: Welcome to Paradise, Population Ten. On the same album in "You're So Beautiful," he narrates how a person was born in paradise, and she is so beautiful that he is in paradise each time he sees her again. If paradise is everything one sees, he concludes, then the place from which his beloved comes is ecstasy.

Paradise, a place or state of perfect happiness, sometimes refers to heaven or the biblical garden of Eden, as it does in "Like a Sad Song." In the Denver repertoire, there are many songs that describe Paradise as mountains and love without mentioning the word *Paradise*.

Scripture: "One of the criminals who were hanged [on either side of the crucified Jesus] kept deriding him and saying, 'Are you not the Messiah? Save yourself and us.' But the other rebuked him, saying, 'Do you not fear God, since you are under the same sentence of condemnation? And we indeed have been condemned justly, for we are getting what we deserve for our deeds, but this man has done nothing wrong.' The he said, 'Jesus, remember me when you come into your kingdom.' He replied, 'Truly I tell you, today you will be with me in Paradise.'" (Luke 23:39–43, NRSV)

Reflection: In biblical literature, there are only eight mentions of the word *Paradise*, and five of those are in the OT (A) book of Second Esdras. Of the other three, there is one each in the CB (NT) in 2 Corinthians 12:4 and Revelation 2:7. The eighth reference is found above in the unique account of Jesus' crucifixion found in Luke's Gospel. In no other gospel do the two co-crucified thieves have speaking parts. The passage presents the bad thief versus the good thief paradigm. The good thief rebukes the bad thief in three ways. He appeals to the healthy fear of God; he makes an affirmation of their common guilt; and he presents Jesus as one not being guilty of anything and unjustly treated. In other words, he makes an act of repentance with the beginning of conversion, a favorite theme of the author of Luke-Acts. Jesus' response to his repentance is to assure him of Paradise that very day. Jesus' use of the word *Paradise* as a place or garden of bliss is echoed in Denver's uses above.

Meditation/Journal: When you read or hear the word *Paradise*, of what do you think? What is your image of Paradise? Explain.

Psalm Response: "[GOD] forgives your sins—every one. / He heals your diseases—every one. / He redeems you . . . —saves your life! / He crowns you with love and mercy—a paradise crown. / He wraps you in goodness—beauty eternal. / He renews your youth—you're always young in his presence. / GOD has set his throne in heaven; / he rules over us all. He's the King! / Bless GOD, all creatures, wherever you are— / everything and everyone made by GOD." (Ps 103:3–5, 19, 22a, TM)

Prayer

JD: The best example of Denver's use of the word *prayer* is found in "Poems, Prayers, and Promises" on the album with the same name. In the song, Denver sings about sitting by a fire and talking of poems and prayers and promises and things believed in by those surrounding the fire. Prayer—communication with God giving thanks, expressing praise, or requesting help—is found in "Friends with You" on the *AER* album; Denver tells his friends that he will pray for them when another day is over, while in "Autograph" on the album with the same name, he urges his listeners to say a prayer and open their hearts again. In "Rhymes and Reasons" on the album with the same name, the song he sings is a prayer to nonbelievers to come and stand with him and find a better way. He calls them prayers up in the sky in "Back Home Again" on the album with the same name. He sings about remembering the moments he prayed that he would never grow old in "Let Us Begin" on the *OW* album, whereas in "Flying for Me" on the same album, he prayed that he would find an answer in the heavens. On the *DD* album in "The Chosen Ones" he asks his listeners to say a prayer for the chosen ones. In "Hold on Tightly" on the *IAT* album, he states that some people pray only for power, while in "Dance Little Jean" on the *FJ* album, he states that a prayer was answered. In "Chained to the Wheel" on the *DD* album, he sings ambiguously about not praying for a sign and praying for a sign! In "Garden Song" on the *JD* album, he tells his listeners to plant their garden rows straight and long and to temper them with a prayer and a song. In "Christmas for Cowboys" on the *RMC* album, he declares that the wind sings a hymn as all bow down to pray. Bowing is the outward sign of a person at prayer. Denver's use of prayer reflect the values of faith, hope, and the simple moments of life. In "Higher Ground" on the album with the same name, a prayer is embedded in the song. He prays that God will keep him through the night, lead him to the light, teach him the magic of wonder, and give him the spirit to fly.

Scripture: "We [—Paul, Silvanus, and Timothy—] always give thanks to God for all of you [Thessalonians] in our prayers, constantly remembering before our God and Father your work of faith and labor of love and steadfastness of hope in our Lord Jesus Christ. For we know, brothers and sisters beloved by God, that he has chosen you, because our message of the gospel came to you not in word only, but also in power and the Holy Spirit and with full conviction; just as you know what kind of persons we proved to be among you for your sake." (1 Thess 1:2–5, NRSV)

Reflection: In Paul's first letter to the Thessalonians—although the letter's greeting indicates that it comes from Paul, Silvanus, and Timothy (1 Thess 1:1)—the apostle indicates that he and his assistants give thanks to God in their prayers for the Thessalonians' work of faith, labor of love, and steadfastness of hope in Jesus Anointed. For Paul, thanksgiving to God is a fundamental attitude indicating the divine initiation in the lives of the Thessalonian believers, whose activity—faith, love, and hope—is mentioned by Paul. The status of chosen is indicated by Paul's reference to them as beloved by God; in other words, Paul's prayer emphasizes the divine character of their election, as demonstrated in their reception of the Spirit and their full conviction to the message of the gospel, as preached by Paul and the co-senders of the letter. Thus, prayer can be thanksgiving, praise, or seeking help. Denver uses all three aspects of prayer, as does Paul.

Meditation/Journal: Make a list of ten things for which you pray. Then, alongside each one indicate if it is thanksgiving, praise, or asking for help for something.

Psalm Response: "I want to drink God, / deep draughts of God. / I'm thirsty for God alive. / I was always . . . / Shouting praises, singing thanksgiving— / celebrating all of us, God's feast! / [I] Fix my eyes on God— / soon I'll be praising again. / He puts a smile on my face, / He's my God. / . . . GOD promises to love me all day, / sing songs all through the night! / My life is God's prayer." (Ps 42:2, 4c, 5b, 8, TM)

Q

Quiet Solitude

JD: Quiet refers to a place where there is little or no noise, and solitude means that one is alone. Thus, in Denver's "Rocky Mountain High" on the album with the same name, the twenty-seven-year-old walks in quiet solitude—alone in the quiet of the mountains—through the forests and the streams seeking grace in every step he takes. Furthermore, the result of quiet solitude is contemplation, or, as Denver sings it, his sight has turned inside himself to try to understand the serenity of a clear blue mountain lake. While serenity is a long time coming to Denver in "Eclipse" on the *ES* album, and he does not know what it means, in "A Little Further North" on *FTSS* album, feeling the night wrap around him eases his mind's serenity. In "The Mountain Song" on the *AUTO* album, Denver echoes the contemplative dimension of the high country, singing about the quiet splendor of a field of columbine. Similarly, in "Cool an' Green an' Shady" on the *BHA* album, some place cool and green and shady is found on a section of grass, upon which one can lie, close one's eyes, find one's self, and lose one's self, while one's free spirit flies. Or in "Song for the Life" on the *AUTO* album, Denver sings about learning how to listen intently and contemplatively for a sound that others cannot hear, like the sound of the sun going down! Thus, quiet solitude for Denver occurs when he is alone in the quiet of nature contemplating the experiences of his life.

Scripture: "The whole earth is at rest and quiet; / they break forth into singing. / The cypresses exult over you, / the cedars of Lebanon, saying, / 'Since you were laid low, / no one comes to cut us down.' / Sheol beneath is stirred up / to meet you when you come; / it rouses the shades to greet you, / all who were leaders of the earth; / it raises from their thrones / all who were kings of the nations. / All of them will speak / and say to you: / 'You too have become as weak as we! / You have become like us!'" (Isa 14:7–10, NRSV)

Reflection: The above passage is out of context. In order to understand it, we must put it back into the context of chapters 13 to 14 of the book of the prophet Isaiah. The above passage is a small part of the prophet's oracle concerning the fall of Babylon. The passage is a mocking lament for the unnamed Babylonian ruler; his power in life is contrasted with his powerlessness in death. According to Isaiah, the LORD has defeated the Babylonian world power, and, thus, the whole earth is quiet. The cypress and cedar trees are singing triumphant songs. Even Sheol, the first level of the then-understood three-storied universe, is ready to receive the Babylonian king. The shades of former earthly rulers who live there will greet the powerful leader by praising his weaknesses! The spirits arise in amazement that such a person so proud and supreme could be brought so low. With the death of the Babylonian king, the earth—the middle story of the three-level universe—breaks into singing of its rest and quiet. In other words, it leads others into contemplation in the quiet experience of the defeat of one of the world's powerful rulers.

Meditation/Journal: In what place do you find quiet solitude? Explain what the serenity is like.

Canticle Response: "God proves to be good to the man who passionately waits, / to the woman who diligently seeks. / It's a good thing to quietly hope, / quietly hope for help from GOD. / It's a good thing when you're young / to stick it out through the hard times. / When life is heavy and hard to take, / go off by yourself. Enter the silence. / Bow in prayer. Don't ask questions: / Wait for hope to appear." (Lam 3:25–29, TM)

R

Rain(bow)

JD: The use of rain in Denver's songs conveys both positive and negative emotions; rain is both good and bad. For example in "Ponies" on the *DD* album, Denver sings that when the storm clouds begin to gather, the ponies run wild before it rains. In "I Remember You" on the *OW* album, he sings about remembering stars that fell from the sky, like the rain comes out of the blue. In "Somethin' About" on the *IAT* album, he says there is something about a rainfall that is like the gift of living. After thinking about the rain in "I'm Sorry" on the *WIND* album, it comes tumbling down in "Garden Song" on the *JD* album. On the *FA* album in "Zachary and Jennifer," he muses that Jennifer will sing in summer showers. On the *SP* album in "Like a Sad Song," he identifies the rain as the sound of heaven singing, and he calls it joyful music.

In "Annie's Song" on the *BHA* album, he sings that she fills up his senses like a walk in the rain. Likewise, in "For Baby (For Bobbie)" on the *RMH* album, he sings that he will walk in the rain by her side. He muses that love may be like thunder when it rains in "Perhaps Love" on the *GH3* album. He promises to give all his sun and rainy days to the one he loves in "True Love Takes Time" on the *OW* album. The hero of "Wild Montana Skies" on the *IAT* album is born in the Bitterroot Valley in the early morning rain. He awakens on most mornings in Alaska to a drizzling rain in "Alaska and Me" on the *HG* album. Denver would rather laugh with the rain in "I'd Rather Be a Cowboy (Lady's Chains)" on the *FA* album. He has seen rain in "Fire and Rain" on the *PPP* album, it is beginning to rain again in "Sweet Melinda" on the *JD* album, and he smelled rain in "Wild Flowers in a Mason Jar (The Farm)" on the *SDD* album. In "A Country Girl in Paris" on the *HG* album, he sings about memories of Nashville, Tennessee, in the rain. However, some people drive the boy from the county into the rain in "Boy from the Country" on the *AEJD* album.

Rain precedes a rainbow, a multi-colored arc of light separated into bands of color—red, orange, yellow, green, blue, indigo, and violet—that appears when the sun's rays are refracted and reflected by drops of rain. In "For Baby (For Bobbie)" on the *RMH* album, Denver says that he will sing the songs of the rainbow. In "Dreamland Express" on the album with the same name, he sings that the person he loves told him to let her be the end of her rainbow. In other words, she is the source of his happiness and joy. In "Rhymes and Reasons" on the album with the same name, Denver compares children to the music of the mountains and the colors of the rainbow. On the rare 1966 *JDS* album in "Anything Love Can Buy," Denver sings about giving the gold at the end of the rainbow to the one he loves. In "The Foxfire Suite: You Are" on the *DD* album, he tells his beloved that she is where the rainbow ends. The wind gives the rain, then it builds a rainbow in "Windsong" on the album with the same name. Thus, a rainbow for Denver, represents the beauty of light and the joy of love. As he states in "Sticky

Summer Weather" on the *TMT* album, he spent a long time looking for rainbows.

Scripture: ". . . [A]s the heavens are higher than the earth, / so are my ways higher than your ways / and my thoughts than your thoughts [, says the LORD]. / For as the rain and the snow come down from heaven, / and do not return there until they have watered the earth, / making it bring forth and sprout, / giving seed to the sower and bread to the eater, / so shall my word be that goes out from my mouth; / it shall not return to me empty, / but it shall accomplish that which I purpose." (Isa 55:9–11, NRSV)

Reflection: The biblical understanding of rain is that it is a gift sent from God, who lives above the dome of the sky in a place called the heavens. Without rain the earth is only dust. However, if one considers the earth as mother and God as father, then in the biblical understanding rain is like the father's sperm that impregnate mother earth, making her fertile and fruitful. Not only does the prophet Isaiah understand rain in this manner, but he also reveals how the heavens manifest that God's ways and thoughts are literally and figuratively higher than human ways and thoughts. Thus, just like rain makes the earth fruitful with seed and bread, so the LORD's word, spoken by the prophet, accomplishes the purpose he intends. What human beings consider to be impossible is possible with God. Thus, while the lyrics of Denver's songs present images of rain compared to various human experiences, Isaiah's image compares the effectiveness of the divine word to the effectiveness of divine male sperm (rain) coming from the heavens to mother earth and giving life wherever it falls.

Meditation/Journal: Is rain negative or positive or both for you? Explain. When you see a rainbow, of what or whom do you think?

Psalm Response: "Oh visit the earth [, God,], / ask her to join the dance! / Deck her out in spring showers, / fill the God-River with living water. / Paint the wheat fields golden. / Creation was made for this! / Drench the plowed fields, / soak the dirt clods / With rainfall as harrow and rake / bring her to blossom and fruit. / Let them shout, and shout, and shout! / Oh, oh, let them sing!" (Ps 65:9–10, 13b, TM)

Ride

JD: Denver uses the word *ride* to refer to travel in a vehicle. For instance he sings about being along for the ride in "Along for the Ride ('56 T-Bird)" on the *OW* album. Similarly, in "Hitchhiker" on the *SP* album, he suggests that the listener pull off to the side of the road and let the old man have a ride. In "Gravel on the Ground" on the *SDD* album, he sings about wishing that life, like a highway, was straight and narrow, then people could see forever before they took the ride, that is before they lived their lives. He sings about riding on the tapestry of everything there is to see in "Season Suite: Spring" on the *RMH* album. In a similar manner, in "On the Wings of a Dream" on the *IAT* album, he asks if this life is just a path to the place from which people have come. Closely associated with ride is road and highway, which are explored below in the road entry. In "Rocky Mountain Suite" on the *FA* album, he sings about two men and four ponies on a long lonesome ride in the Canadian Rockies, riding horses. Similarly, in "Song of Wyoming" on the *WIND* album, he sings about being weary, tired, and finished with his day's ride.

Scripture: ". . . I [, John of Patmos,] saw heaven opened, and there was a white horse! Its rider is called Faithful and True, and in righteousness he judges and makes war. His eyes are like a flame of fire, and on his head are many diadems; and he has a name inscribed that no one knows but himself. He is clothed in a robe dipped in blood, and his name is called The Word of God. On his robe and on his thigh he has a name inscribed, 'King of kings and Lord of lords.'" (Rev 19:11–13, 16, NRSV)

Reflection: While most of Denver's references to ride concern the vehicle of a car—which had not yet been invented when the biblical books were written—the biblical writers, like Denver in "Rocky Mountain Suite," knew ride in terms of mounting a horse. Thus, at the end of the book of Revelation in the CB (NT), the heavenly warrior rides a white horse; his victory will bring an end to the war launched by the dragon earlier in the story. The rider is, of course, Jesus, who was described earlier in the book as being faithful and true. There is no doubt that he is divine, as he, like God, is described as fire. His bloody robe indicates that he has won the victory over the dragon and over death. Indeed, his name—the Word of God—indicates how he has won the victory. He has a tattoo on his thigh revealing him to be the King of kings and the Lord of lords. His ride on a white horse is the victory lap after leading the armies of heaven—clothed in white linen and riding on white horses—to victory over the wicked.

Meditation/Journal: When you hear the word *ride*, of what do you think? Explain.

Psalm Response: "My heart bursts its banks, / spilling beauty and goodness. / I pour it out in a poem to the king, / shaping the river into words: / 'You're the handsomest of men; / every word from your lips is sheer grace, /

and God has blessed you, blessed you so much. / Strap your sword to your side, warrior! / Accept praise! Accept due honor! / Ride majestically! Rule Triumphantly! / Ride on the side of truth! / Ride for the righteous meek!'" (Ps 45:1–4, TM)

River

JD: In "Take Me Home, Country Roads" on the *PPP* album, Denver names the Shenandoah River, located in the western part of Virginia. In the same song, he mentions the Blue Ridge Mountains, located in the eastern panhandle of West Virginia at the confluence of the Shenandoah and Potomac rivers. The song stands as a tribute to the beauty of the region, Denver's personal experience, and Denver's appreciation for nature. In "In the Grand Way" on the *SP* album, he sings about mountain rivers; in "Song of Wyoming" on the *WIND* album, he watches the river roll by; in "The Flower That Shattered the Stone" on the *ES* album, the river runs freely; and in "Mother Nature's Son" on the *RMH* album, he sits beside a mountain stream and watches the water rise. In "Chained to the Wheel" on the *DD* album, he refers to red rivers of fire and steel, a likely reference to the rivers of molten steel poured out of a steel-making plant. While commentators think he is referring to the Colorado River in "Amazon" on the *DD* album, he sings about a river that runs from the mountains, and that one river is all rivers and all rivers are that one. It is the river of no regret, he sings, and adds, let this be a voice for the river. He does not name the river in the song. The state of Alaska calls him to the rivers, where he can be strong, in "To the Wild Country" on the *ES* album. In "Pegasus" on the *SP* album, he sings about rivers dark with sound; these are endless rivers of love. In "All of My Memories" on the *AER* album, he mentions the sweet singing river. In "Alaska and Me" on the *HG* album, he sings about sleeping near the sound of a slow-running river. The 1988 Theme Song for the Global Forum, "The One World," expresses his perspective that the one world in which we live is meant to be shared, including its rivers. Finally, in "Downhill Stuff" on the *JD* album he sings that some people keep moving like a river rolling toward the sea.

In "What's on Your Mind" on the *JD* album, he compares what is on one's mind to catching a ride on a beautiful river, which will carry all away. And in "River" on the *HG* album, the whole song is a metaphor using river to sing about his separation from his beloved.

Scripture: "Naaman, commander of the army of the king of Aram, was a great man and in high favor with his master, because by him the LORD had given victory to Aram. The man, though a mighty warrior, suffered from leprosy. . . . Naaman came with his horses and chariots, and halted at the entrance of Elisha's house. Elisha sent a messenger to him, saying, 'Go, wash in the Jordan [River] seven times, and your flesh shall be restored and you shall be clean.' [Naaman asked,] "Are not Abana [River] and Pharpar [River], the rivers of Damascus, better than all the waters of Israel? Could I not wash in them, and be clean?'. . . [Naaman] went down and immersed himself seven times in the Jordan, according to the word of the man of God; his flesh was restored like the flesh of a young boy, and he was clean." (2 Kgs 5:1, 9–10, 12, 14, NRSV)

Reflection: The above story is extracted from a much longer account found in the HB (OT) Second Book of Kings (5:1–27). The main character is the Syrian army commander Naaman, who had become a leper. His king sent him to the king of Israel, who in turn sent him to the prophet Elisha, who told him to dunk himself in the Jordan seven times to precipitate a cure. At first Naaman was angry, because he had hoped for some sign from Elisha that invoked the LORD. However, Elisha gave no such sign. Naaman reflected that the two major rivers of his home country were cleaner than the Jordan River, but after being urged by members of his staff to reconsider his position of not following Elisha's orders, he went to the Jordan, plunged himself in seven times, and emerged cured! In other words, the river water washed away Naaman's disease. The Jordan River was holy water! After returning to Elisha, who rejected his gifts, Naaman asked for two mule-loads of earth to take with him to Syria, so he could worship the LORD on God's soil. In the biblical world, rivers serve as boundaries both for countries and to separate the sacred from the profane. Denver sings about rivers being signs of life rolling along.

Meditation/Journal: What is your favorite river? What does it represent or signify for you? Explain.

Psalm Response: "River fountains splash joy, cooling God's city, / this sacred haunt of the Most High. / God lives here, the streets are safe, / God at your service from crack of dawn. / Godless nations rant and rave, kings and kingdoms threaten, / but Earth does anything he says. / Attention, all! See the marvels of GOD!" (Ps 46:4–6, 8a, TM)

Road

JD: For Denver, the word *road* is a metaphor for life's journey and the search for meaning. In "Take Me Home, Country Roads" on the *PPP* album, the road brings him back to his roots or home and a simple way of life. Not only does the title indicate that he is traveling a country road, but he sings about driving down the road. In "Gravel on the Ground" on the *SDD* album, he tells the listeners that they should walk the road together; who knows what they will find the next day. One person is always on the road in "Two Different Directions" on the *DD* album, while in "On the Road" on the *BHA* album, he sings about just being on the road. Also, on the same album, he sings about ten days on the road being barely gone in "Back Home Again." Driving down the road in "Hitchhiker" on the *SP* album, can be an adventure; it's not a bad life on the road with wheels to roll in "Baby, You Look Good to Me Tonight" on the *SP* album. On the road of experience in "Looking for Space" on the *WIND* album, Denver sings about looking for space to find out who he is. It's a long hard road from across the water to Carolina in "The Foxfire Suite: Spring Is Alive" on the *DD* album. In "True Love Takes Time" on the *OW* album, he travels down the road of true love, a road he has traveled before; he states everyone has traveled that road.

Closely associated with road in Denver's songs is highway, the only home the old hitchhiker knows in "Hitchhiker" on the *SP* album. He is lost and alone on some forgotten highway in "Sweet Surrender" on the *BHA* album, while he states that he has been out on a highway for five days in a row in "Baby, You Look Good to Me Tonight" on the *SP* album; he has been on the highway a long time in "On the Wings of an Eagle" on the *FJ* album; and he is king of the highway in "Along for the Ride ('56 T-Bird)" on the *OW* album. In "Gravel on the Ground" on the *SDD* album, it is a straight and narrow highway. In "River" on the *FJ* album, he states that running away just changes the view of the highway. He says that his future is killing him in "To the Wild Country" on the *ES* album, because it is a misbegotten highway of prophecies and dreams, a road to nowhere and eternity. Similarly, he asks about the highway to heaven in "Hold on Tightly" on the *IAT* album, and says that it is a highway without any end in "We Don't Live Here No More" on the *FA* album. In "All of My Memories" on the *AER* album, he states that his memories are about life on the highway with nights in old motels, while sleeping alone. In "Gravel on the Ground" on the *SDD* album, he declares that life is not an easy freeway.

Scripture: ". . . Balaam got up in the morning, saddled his donkey, and went with the officials of Moab. . . . [T]he angel of the LORD took his stand in the road as his adversary. Now he was riding on the donkey, and his two servants were with him. The donkey saw the angel of the LORD standing in the road, with a drawn sword in his hand; so the donkey turned off the road, and went into the field; and Balaam struck the donkey, to turn it back onto the road. Then the angel of the LORD stood in a narrow path between the vineyards, with a wall on either side. When the donkey saw the angel of the LORD, it scraped Balaam's foot against the wall; so he struck it again. Then the angel of the LORD went ahead, and stood in a narrow place, where there was no way to turn either to the right or to the left. When the donkey saw the angel of the LORD, it lay down under Balaam; and Balaam's anger was kindled, and he struck the donkey with his staff. Then the LORD opened the mouth of the donkey and it said to Balaam, 'What have I done to you, that you have struck me these three times?'" (Num 22:21–29, NRSV)

Reflection: The elders of Moab and Midian go to Balaam, living on the Euphrates River, to get him to come with them to curse the Israelites, who have just emerged out of Egyptian slavery. However, God, who has sworn to protect the Israelites, tells Balaam not to go. After a second attempt by the elders, God tells him to go with the men, but to do only what he tells him to do. On the road to Moab, Balaam's donkey stops three times, and Balaam beats it three times. Any reader knowing ancient numerology immediately sees that God, in the person of an angel, has appeared to Balaam. God tells him to go with Balak, king of Moab, but to speak only what God tells him. Balak wants Balaam to curse the Israelites; a biblical curse is supposed to destroy those upon whom it is uttered. Every time Balaam opens his mouth to curse the Israelites, God intervenes, and Balaam ends up blessing them—four times!—before, finally, leaving and going back home. Thus, God's people are blessed by a prophet who was brought to curse them!

Meditation/Journal: Like Balaam, have you ever encountered God on a road? Narrate the experience.

Decree Response: "Decree of Balam son of Beor, / decree of the man with 20/20 vision, / Decree of the man who hears godly speech, / who knows what's going on with the High God, / Who sees what The Strong God reveals, / who bows in worship and sees what's real. / I see him, but not right now, / I perceive him, but not right here; / A star rises from Jacob / a scepter from Israel . . . . / A ruler is coming from Jacob . . . ." (Num 24:15–17, 19a, TM)

S

Season(s)

JD: Denver uses the word *season(s)* in the titles of two songs: "Season Suite" on the *Rocky Mountain High* album and "Seasons of the Heart" on the album with the same name. In "Season Suite: Spring," he asks the hearer if he or she can see himself or herself reflected in the seasons. And in "Seasons of the Heart," he sings about the differences between people that are as natural as changes in the seasons. In "Season Suite," Denver is acknowledging the four seasons literally, providing lyrics that describe the natural world during each season. However, in "Seasons of the Heart," he is using seasons metaphorically to signify the cyclical nature of life, love, and relationships and the emotions accompanying those stages.

Scripture: ". . . God said, 'Let there be lights in the dome of the sky to separate the day from the night; and let them be for signs and for seasons and for days and years, and let them be lights in the dome of the sky to give light upon the earth.' And it was so. God made the two great lights—the greater light to rule the day and the lesser light to rule the night—and the stars. God set them in the dome of the sky to give light upon the earth, to rule over the day and over the night, and to separate the light from the darkness. And God saw that it was good. And there was evening and there was morning, the fourth day." (Gen 1:14–19, NRSV)

Reflection: The above passage is from the first account of creation found in the HB (OT) book of Genesis (1:1—2:3). The first three days of creation in that story form the three regions of the ancient conception of the world as a three-level universe. On the first day God separates the light from the darkness, even though he doesn't create the region of the sky (dome) until the second day, and the sources of light until the third day, when he also creates the plate-like structure called earth. While it is not in this account, the first level of the universe is called Sheol; it is where the dead live, as contrasted to the earth, where people live, and above the dome, where God lives. The author of the account reveals his understanding that a day begins on the evening before the next morning, which is not the contemporary understanding that a day begins at midnight and ends seconds before the next midnight, when a new day begins. Ancient biblical people used the sun and especially the moon to calculate their annual seasons and feasts.

Meditation/Journal: What role do the sun and moon play in your calculation of annual seasons and feasts?

Psalm Response: "The moon keeps track of the seasons, / the sun is in charge of each day. / When it's dark and night takes over, / all the forest creatures come out. / When the sun comes up, [the young lions] vanish, / lazily stretched out in their dens. / Meanwhile, men and women go out to work, / busy at their jobs until evening. / What a wildly wonder world, GOD! / You made it all, with Wisdom at your side, / made earth overflow with your wonderful creations." (Ps 104:19–20, 22–24, TM)

Snow

JD: While snow is mentioned in several of Denver's songs, snow is most mentioned in "The Blizzard," a version of Judy Collins' song with the same name and sent to her as a demo, but never released by Denver. The song, recorded in the 1990s, was released in 2017 to commemorate the twentieth anniversary of Denver's death. In "The Blizzard," Denver sings about how it started to snow, how the snow flies, how the white powder becomes a snowfall, and how the snow continued to fall. He explains how he followed a stranger through the snow, how the sun shined on the snow the next morning, how his car was buried in six feet of snow drifts, and how the snow plow removed it from the road. In "Two Shots" on the *WIND* album, he sings about the sound of snow softly falling, while in "Aspenglow" on the *TMT* album, he dreams of softly falling snow, and in "Whalebones and Crosses" on the *AUTO* album, he sings about eternal snow that covers the graves in the cemetery. In "Love Is the Master" on the *OW* album, he states that there will be snow on the passes, because he can feel it in the chill of the wind. The snow-covered hills, in "Starwood in Aspen" on the *AER* album, get him to thinking about his home named Starwood and his friends, who are the snow-covered hills. In "Season Suite: Winter" on the *RMH* album, he sings that the snow is trying to get him down. Similarly, in "High Wind Blowin'" on the *FJ* album, Denver is upset because it was snowing in his bed. Thus, for Denver, snow is an exhilarating experience, although too much of it can depress him.

Scripture: "By [the Most High's] command he sends the driving snow . . . . Therefore the storehouses are opened, / and the clouds fly out like birds. / He scatters the snow like birds flying down / and its descent is like locusts alighting. / The eye is dazzled by the beauty of its whiteness, / and the mind is amazed as it falls. (Sir 43:13a, 14, 17c–18, NRSV)

Reflection: Actual experiences with snow were rare for biblical people. While it might snow in Jerusalem occasionally, the usual experience of snow was seeing it on mountain tops. Biblical people presumed that God Most High possessed storehouses above the dome of the sky in which he kept natural forces, like snow. As is noted in the passage from the OT (A) book of Sirach, snow with the sun shining on it represented God's glory, because it was rare, exotic, resplendent, and noteworthy. For Denver, living in the mountains of Aspen, Colorado, snow was commonplace throughout the winter and on mountain tops at times during the spring, summer, and fall.

Meditation/Journal: What are your experiences of snow? Make a list and describe how each made you feel.

Psalm Response: "Hallelujah! / It's a good thing to sing praise to our God; / praise is beautiful, praise is fitting. / He spreads snow like a white fleece, / he scatters frost like ashes . . . . / Then he gives the command and it all melts; / he breathes on winter—suddenly it's spring!" (Ps 147:1, 16, 18, TM)

Song

JD: Denver uses the word *song* in several titles for songs; among those include "Wrangle Mountain Song," "The Mountain Song," and "Song for the Life" on the *AUTO* album, "Annie's Song" on the *BHA* album, "Song of Wyoming" on the *WIND* album, and "Eli's Song" and "Like a Sad Song" on the *SP* album. There are two album titles that contain the word *song*: *Windsong* and *Earth Songs*.

In "This Old Guitar" on the *BHA* album, Denver sings that the old guitar taught him to sing a love song, to sing other songs, and the fact that he loves to sing his songs, as demonstrated in "Matthew"—on the same album—in which he sings that it is for Matthew that the song is sung. There is a song for the life he has found in "Song for the Life" on the *AUTO* album, and there's a song for a friend he found in the same song on the same album. In "Rocky Mountain High" on the album with the same name, Denver sings that the twenty-seven-year-old's life was hanging by a song before he came to the mountains. On the same album in "For Baby (For Bobbie)," he offers to sing the songs of the rainbow, while in "Cowboy's Delight" on the *WIND* album, he sings the songs of the sunrise into the night. Also on the *WIND* album in "Song of Wyoming," he sings that it is a song of Wyoming for him. In "Fire and Rain" on the *PPP* album, he explains that he awakened one morning and wrote down the song, whereas in "Farewell Andromeda" on the album with the same name, he declares that all the songs he plays are to thank a person for allowing him into the lovely day he or she made. Similarly, in "Today" on the *AEJD* album, he sings that people will know who he is by the songs that he sings. On the *PPP* album in "Sunshine on My Shoulders," he states if he had a song that he could sing for his listeners, he would sing one that would make them feel the sunshine high he feels. In "Leaving on a Jet Plane" on the *R&R* album, he declares that every song he sings he sings for the person he loves. Does the heart know the way, and, if not, can the path be found in a song, he asks in "On the Wings of a Dream" on the *IAT* album; he adds that truth can be found in a song. In "Eli's Song" on the *SP* album he sings that Eli likes to sing songs, while in "Like a Sad Song" on the same album, he sings that sometimes he feels like a sad song. In "San Antonio Rose" on the *SP* album, he sings a song of old San Antone, while he fills the silence with a song in "A Wild Heart Looking for Home" on the *DE* album. No more songs of the hunters on the buffalo plain are heard in "Trail of Tears" on the *DE* album. On the *R&R* album, there is the one-line song—"The Ballad of Spiro Agnew"—in which Denver sings a song of Spiro Agnew! On the *DE* album in "Amazon," Denver summarizes his use of the word *song*, singing that one song encompasses all music, and all songs are that one song of life. Similarly, in "Songs of . . ." on the *JD* album, he summarizes that there are songs of the future, past, first day, last day, tomorrow, play, struggles, and the way. Finally, in "Windsong" on the album with the same name, he declares that it was the wind which sang the first song; also, the wind knows the songs of the cities and the canyons.

Scripture: "The waters [of the Red Sea] returned and covered the chariots and the chariot drivers, the entire army of Pharaoh that had followed [the Israelites] into the sea; not one of them remained. But the Israelites walked on dry ground through the sea, the waters forming a wall for them on their right and on their left. Thus the LORD saved Israel that day from the Egyptians, and Israel saw the Egyptians dead on the seashore. Israel saw the great work that the LORD did against the Egyptians. So the people feared the LORD and believed in the LORD and in his servant Moses. Then Moses and the Israelites sang this song to the LORD: 'I will sing to the LORD, for he has triumphed gloriously; / horse and rider he has thrown into the sea.'" (Exod 14:28—15:1, NRSV)

Reflection: The key event in the HB (OT) is the Hebrews' escape from Egyptian slavery by passing through the Red Sea or Sea of Reeds. The biblical event illustrates the LORD's power over the chaos of water; in the narrative after he tells Moses to extend his hand over the sea and split it in two, after Moses and the Israelites cross through the sea on dry ground, Moses extends his hand over the sea and reverses the process. The LORD not only saves his chosen people, but he defeats their enemy by drowning Pharaoh's chariots, chariot drivers, and army (not to mention the horses pulling the chariots). As the Israelites see the bodies of the Egyptians and the remnants of their chariots floating in the water, they attribute the Egyptian defeat and their victory to the LORD; they call it a work of God. It inspires divine awe in them, and strengthens their faith in the LORD and their trust in Moses, God's servant. Then, after witnessing the event, they break into song. After experiencing events, Denver writes songs about what he has experienced.

Meditation/Journal: What do you consider to be the greatest event you have ever witnessed? What song do you associate with the event?

Canticle Response: "I'm singing my heart out to GOD—what a victory! / He pitched horse and rider into the sea. / GOD is my strength, GOD is my song, / and, yes! GOD is my salvation. / *This* is the kind of God I have / and I'm telling the world! / *This* is the God of my father— / I'm spreading the news far and wide! / GOD is a fighter, / pure GOD, through and through. / Pharaoh's chariots and army / he dumped in the sea. / Wild ocean waters poured over them; / they sank like a rock in the deep blue sea. / Your strong right hand, GOD, shimmers with power; / your strong right hand shatters the enemy." (Exod 15:1b–4a, 5–6, TM)

(Great) Spirit

JD: Denver has an album titled *SP* with the song titled "The Wings that Fly Us Home." In that song he sings about the spirit filling the darkness of the heavens and the endless yearning of the soul, and the spirit lives within a star too far of which to dream and within each part and in the whole. The last phrase—within each part and in the whole—illustrates an underlying presupposition of many of Denver's songs, known as the concept of nonduality. While many people unconsciously live in a dual universe, meaning that they separate themselves from everything, Denver sings about the unity of all people and things. Nonduality means feeling one with others and things and engaging with them nonviolently. In general, people resist nonduality because it challenges their perceived privilege and power. Using the spirit that permeates everything, Denver attempts to erase the blindness that excuses the separation between people, animals, and things. The spirit binds all together, he sings in "Islands" on the *SH* album. Also, Denver has a song titled "Spirit" on the *WIND* album. That song begins with his— there is no antecedent noun—and continues to narrate that his spirit joined and formed the wind ten thousand years ago. In "Trail of Tears" on the *DE* album, Denver sings about the children of Native Americans who will not learn the ways of the Great Spirit.

In "Sweet Surrender" on the *BHA* album, Denver sings about there being a spirit that guides him. In "Windsong" on the album with the same name, he urges his listeners to let the breezes surround them in their hearts and in their spirits. On the same album, he sings to the spirit of Calypso in the song "Calypso." In "Higher Ground" on the album with the same name he asks for the spirit to fly, while in "Flying for Me" on the *OW* album, he praises the astronauts in the Challenger disaster for having given their spirit, especially Christa McAuliffe, about whom Denver sings that she gave her spirit. While he sings in "Eagles & Horses" on *FTSS* album that his spirit would never be broken or caught, in "In My Heart" on the *AUTO* album, he sings about the beautiful weather breaking his spirit and tearing apart his mind. When needing someone beside him, his spirit must be strong, sings Denver in "What One Man Can Do" on the *SH* album. In "The Gold and Beyond" on the *GH3* album, he says that his spirit is burning, consumed by the flame to be one of the best in the world. In "Joseph & Joe" on the *JD* album, he explains how Joseph can put one in touch with the spirit of man and woman. Denver's summary concerning spirit is found in "All This Joy" on the *HG* album. All joy, sorrow, promise, and pain are part of life, being, love, and spirit.

Scripture: "The human spirit is the lamp of the LORD, / searching every inmost part." (Prov 20:27, NRSV)

Reflection: Every person possesses spirit; the Hebrew word *ruah* can be translated as spirit, breath, and wind, depending upon its context. Because a human being has the breath (spirit) of life blown into his or her nostrils by God (Gen 2:7), whereby he or she becomes a living being, a human is like a divine lamp spreading God's light everywhere. Furthermore, because everyone is inspirited, self-awareness becomes a share in God's intelligence and it gives people the ability to understand themselves and judge themselves, what today would be called conscience. Thus, the power or ability to know oneself and articulate it is to share in the LORD's spirit. When Denver sings that the spirit lives within each part and is the whole in "The Wings That Fly Us Home" on the *SP* album, he is expressing the same sentiment as the proverb above.

Meditation/Journal: Characterize your spirit; what is your spirit like? Explain how you know and experience your spirit. Explain how you know and experience others' spirit. Are those experiences the same as the LORD's spirit? Explain.

Psalm Response: "I'm an open book to you [, GOD,]; / even from a distance, you know what I'm thinking. / You know when I leave and when I get back; / I'm never out of your sight. / Is there anyplace I can go to avoid your Spirit? / to be out of your sight? / If I climb to the sky, you're there! / If I go underground, you're there! / If I flew on morning's wings, / to the far western horizon, / You'd find me in a minute— / you're already there waiting!" (Ps 139:2, 7–10, TM)

Spring(time)

JD: In "Whispering Jesse" on the *HG* album, Denver sings about always having loved springtime, the passing of winter, the green of the new leaves on the trees, and life going on. This is seen in "The Foxfire Suite: Spring Is Alive" on the *DD* album; Denver begins by announcing that spring is alive in Carolina deep in the forest, high on a mountain, and down in a holler. In "Season Suite: Spring" on the *RMH* album, he declares that the earth has been reborn and life goes on; there is no mention of spring other than in the title of the subsection, just like there is in "Season Suite: Late Winter, Early Spring (When Everybody Goes to Mexico)." In "Annie's Song" on the *BHA* album, Denver, presumably, tells Annie that she fills up his senses like the mountains in springtime. With no noun-antecedent for she in "Fly Away" on the *WIND* album, Denver states that she is looking for signs of the spring. Springtime rolls around slowly in "Starwood in Aspen" on the *AER* album. And a warm wind from the south brings the first taste of spring in "Wild Montana Skies" on the *IAT* album. There is something about the country on the very first day of springtime, sings Denver in "Somethin' About" on the *IAT* album. In "Gimme Your Love" on the *DE* album, Denver sings that spring has arrived and love is in the air overflowing with life. He mentions the signs of rebirth, resurrection, and renewal as he celebrates earthly life. Denver's beloved is a gift, like the very first breath of spring, in "The Gift You Are" on *FTSS* album. While he cannot live on the promises of winter to spring in "Today" on *AEJD* album, he states that if he could have one wish, it would be to see another spring and bless the falling leaves, a metaphor for refugees in "Falling Leaves (The Refugees)" on the *HG* album. Finally, Denver declares that it is a sad song to sing about the green fading picture of spring in "Rusty Green" on the *FJ* album. Nevertheless, in the springtime the rain is sweet and the wind is cool and clear in "Sticky Summer Weather" on the *TMT* album. And, of course, everyone must remember that one plants tomatoes in the spring in "Home Grown Tomatoes" on the *HG* album.

Scripture: "Hear this, O foolish and senseless people, / who have eyes, but do not see, / who have ears, but do not hear. / Do you not fear me? says the LORD; / They do not say in their hearts, 'Let us fear the LORD our God, / who gives the rain in its season, / the autumn rain and the spring rain, / and keeps for us / the weeks appointed for the harvest.'" (Jer 5:21–22a, 24, NRSV)

Reflection: For ancient biblical people, the important seasons were those marked by rain: autumn and spring (Hos 6:3). In the above passage from Jeremiah, the prophet regards the Israelites as foolish and senseless, because they are not responding positively to the LORD their God. They do not reflect (see, hear) upon their need to be in awe of the God who led them out of Egyptian slavery and into the land he promised to their forefather Abraham. Easily, they forget that the LORD sends them rain in both the spring and the autumn; the rain enables them to gather their harvest during the appointed weeks. Through their ability to see and to hear rain, they should conclude that they need to thank (fear) God for his blessings to them. In other words, just as the rains come regularly, God desires that his chosen people be regular in their faithfulness to and worship of the LORD, and in justice shown to others.

Meditation/Journal: What does the season of spring mean to you?

Psalm Response: "[GOD,] Why not help us make a fresh start—a resurrection life? / *Then* your people will laugh and sing! / Show us how much you love us, GOD! / Give us the salvation we need! / Love and Truth meet in the street, / Right Living and Whole Living embrace and kiss! / Truth sprouts green from the ground, / Right Living pours down from the skies! / Oh yes! GOD gives Goodness and Beauty; / our land responds with Bounty and Blessing." (Ps 85:6–7, 10–12, TM)

Star(light)

JD: In "Rocky Mountain High" on the album with the same name, Denver sings that the shadow from the starlight is softer than a lullaby. The lyrics present a poetic reflection on an experience of being in the mountains at night. In "And I Love Her" on the *JDS* album, he states that the stars that shine are bright at night, another experience had only in the high country. In "Catch Another Butterfly" on the *R&R* album, he mentions that the nights were full of stars, which were there for the wishing. And in "Earth Day Every Day (Celebrate)" on the *ES* album, he urges listeners to celebrate evening, defined as the stars that appear in the sky with the loss of the sun.

In "Shanghai Breezes" on the *GH3* album, he explains that the stars seen in Shanghai are, in general, the same ones seen anywhere around the world.

Denver's other use of star conveys emotion and is often used metaphorically. For example, he guesses his lucky star fell the day the person he loves came along in "Thanks to You" on *FTSS* album. In "Flying for Me" on the *OW* album, he sings about wanting to dance upon a falling star. In "The Foxfire Suite: You Are" on the *DD* album, he sings that the person he loves is where the stars are shining. In "The Flower That Shattered the Stone" on the *ES* album, he compares pure love to a bright star in heaven that lights our way home. He urges people to sing for all the stars above in "Falling Leaves (The Refugees)" on the *HG* album. In "The One World" the Theme Song Denver wrote for the Global Forum in 1988, he names the earth as the one star of all stars; it is the star that is wished on every night; it is a star with its own special light. Only one song features the word star in the title, and that is "Starwood in Aspen" on the *AER* album. Starwood is the name Denver gave to his home on a side of a mountain near Aspen, Colorado.

Scripture: Jesus said to his disciples: ". . . [B]e alert; . . . [I]n those days, after that suffering, the sun will be darkened, / and the moon will not give its light, / and the stars will be falling from heaven, / and the powers in the heavens will be shaken. Then they will see 'the Son of Man coming in clouds' with great power and glory." (Mark 13:23a, 24–26, NRSV)

Reflection: The above verses are taken from chapter 13 of Mark's Gospel, and they are part of a larger passage known as the Little Apocalypse. Apocalypse is a Greek word meaning to uncover or to reveal. While such material is usually pessimistic concerning the present world, it describes events to take place in the future using already-experienced earthly phenomena. For example, the darkening of the sun is an eclipse of the sun; the darkening of the moon is a lunar eclipse. Stars falling out of the sky are meteorites. The shaking of the powers in the heavens can be a severe thunder storm or a tornado. The coming of the Son of Man (a human being) is borrowed from the prophet Daniel (7:13) and suggests a messiah (anointed) Davidic figure who will rule the world as king. Once Christians adopted the HB (OT), they considered that ruler to be Jesus Anointed (Christ), whom they thought was returning soon. While apocalyptic literature is usually dualistic and full of ancient signs—like stars falling from the sky—it urges its readers to be steadfast; the divine will soon enter human history again to reward the righteous and punish the wicked. The CB (NT) contains a whole book written in codes that tell that story: Book of Revelation. Such apocalyptic signs—like stars falling from the sky (meteorites)—are safe signs, because meteorites are bombarding the earth quite frequently; thus, they herald the divine presence constantly.

Meditation/Journal: What do stars represent for you? Are they merely meteorites, or do they convey emotions? Explain.

Psalm Response: "Hallelujah! / Praise GOD from heaven, / praise him from the mountaintops; / Praise him, all you his angels, / praise him, all you his warriors, / Praise him, sun and moon, / praise him, you morning stars; / Praise him, high heaven, / praise him, heavenly rain clouds; / Praise, oh let them praise the name of GOD— / he spoke the word, and there they were! (Ps 148:1–5, TM)

Storm

JD: In Denver's song lyrics, the word *storm* is used primarily in two ways. First, the word is used to describe an event in nature. In "Back Home Again" on the album with the same name, Denver begins the song by stating that there is a storm across the valley and clouds are rolling in. Similarly, in "Annie's Song" on the *BHA* album, he tells her that she fills up his senses like a storm in the desert. And in "Calypso" on the *WIND* album, he sings about riding on the crest of a wild, raging storm at sea. Each of the three songs also uses storm to express more. For example, the storm across the valley in "Back Home Again" represents the longing and weariness of travel and contrasts to the comfort and warmth of returning home. Filling up his senses like a storm in the desert indicates the depth of his love. Riding the crest of a wild, raging storm at sea embodies the thrill and unpredictability of exploration and adventure and reflects Denver's admiration for the daring spirit of those who venture into the unknown world of the ocean.

Second, the word *storm* is used as a metaphor. In "Wild Montana Skies" on the *IAT* album, the young man rides a storm across the mountains; the storm is a metaphor for the man's life from the age of twenty-one to thirty. After leaving home and experiencing the ways of the world—the storm—he returns to Montana to farm the land. In "Perhaps Love" on the *GH3* album, Denver conjectures that love is like a resting place, a shelter from a storm. Life's hardships and emotional turmoil—storms—find shelter, comfort, and protection in a love relationship. Joseph and Joe meet for a time between storms in "Joseph & Joe" on the *JD* album; the priest and the cowboy are on the side of a mountain. Thus, for Denver a storm can be a natural occurrence or it can be a metaphor mirroring the chaos of life.

Scripture: "A jealous . . . God is the LORD . . . . / His way is in whirlwind and storm, / and the clouds are the dust of his feet. / He rebukes the sea and makes it dry, / and he dries up all the rivers . . . . / The mountains quake before him, / and the hills melt; / the earth heaves before him, / the world and all who live in it." (Nah 1:2a, 3b–4a, 5, NRSV)

Reflection: In biblical literature, God often appears in the form of a thunderstorm (Exod 19:17–17), as he does in the passage from the minor prophet Nahum above. Furthermore, his appearance shakes the world of nature (Mic 1:3–4). In biblical literature, God commands the waters of the sea (Gen 1:9), unlike Baal, a storm and fertility god in Near Eastern mythology, whose traditional enemy was the sea. Because ancient people feared storms and their power, they thought of them as manifesting the LORD God. Such a natural occurrence as a storm became charged with divine presence in biblical literature, just as Denver takes the natural occurrence of a storm and uses it to represent the chaos of life in the lyrics of his songs.

Meditation/Journal: Other than being an occurrence of nature, what does a storm represent for you? Explain.

Psalm Response: "O God! Your way is holy! / No god is great like God! / You're the God who makes things happen; / you showed everyone what you can do— / Ocean saw you in action, God, / saw you and trembled with fear; / Deep Ocean was scared to death. / Clouds belched buckets of rain, / Sky exploded with thunder, / your arrows flashing this way and that. / From Whirlwind came your thundering voice, / Lightning exposed the world, / Earth reeled and rocked. / You strode right through Ocean, / walked straight through roaring Ocean, / but nobody saw you come or go." (Ps 77:13–14, 16–19, TM)

Summer

JD: For Denver, the season of summer is desired during the winter, but when it arrives, it is hot. He sings about always loving the long days of summer in "Whispering Jesse" on the *HG* album. He knows that it is more than worth the waiting during the winter for another chance to see the summer sun in "Season Suite: Winter" on the *RMH* album. And while he believes that summer is here to stay in "Season Suite: Summer" on the same album, he laments having three months of summer with nothing to do in "Southwind" on the *JD* album, because sticky summer weather always pains him; it is like living beneath a blanket and not being able to breathe in "Sticky Summer Weather" on the *TMT* album. Also, Jessie went away during the summer in

"I'd Rather Be a Cowboy (Lady's Chains)" on the *FA* album, and, thus, the summer is almost gone in "Rusty Green" on the *FJ* album. Not to be forgotten is the twenty-seven-year-old who was (re)born in the summer in "Rocky Mountain High" on the album with the same name. In "The Foxfire Suite: You Are" on the *DD* album, he sings that his beloved is all summer flowers. And as everyone knows, one eats homegrown tomatoes in the summer in "Home Grown Tomatoes" on the *HG* album. As already noted, the titles of two songs contain the word *summer*: "Season Suite: Summer" and "Sticky Summer Weather."

Scripture: "Go to the ant, you lazybones; / consider its ways, and be wise. / Without having any chief / or officer or ruler, / it prepares its food in summer, / and gathers its sustenance in harvest. / How long will you lie there, O Lazybones? / When will you rise from your sleep? [T]he ants are a people without strength, / yet they provide their food in the summer." (Prov 6:6–9; 30:25, NRSV)

Reflection: The author of the HB (OT) book of Proverbs offers a lesson to be learned by the lazy from the ant in the summer. By observing and reflecting on the ant's ways, a person can gain wisdom. According to author (who turns out to be wrong), ants do not have a boss, yet they gather, prepare, and store their food during the summer. Furthermore, they have little strength (another incorrect observation), but they are strong enough to gather, prepare, and store food. In other words, for the ant summer is a busy time; weak ants are energetic and responsible during the summer. It is a very common sight during the summer to see either ants in a line traveling from one place to another or small mounds of earth that they have excavated. Their pheromone trails guide ants to food, and their well-organized colonies send workers to harvest the food and bring it back to their underground home one piece at a time. In their underground chambers eggs are laid, larvae are hatched and raised, and fed. Unlike Denver, who considers summer too hot to accomplish anything, ants take full advantage of the season to prepare for winter.

Meditation/Journal: What does the season of summer mean or represent to you? Explain.

Canticle Response: "There's an opportune time to do things, a right time for everything on the earth: A right time for birth and another for death, / A right time to plant and another to reap, / A right time to kill and another to heal, / A right time to destroy and another to construct, / A right time to cry and another to laugh, / A right time to lament and another to cheer, / A right time to make love and another to abstain, / A right time to embrace and another to part, / A right time to search and another to count your losses, / A right time to hold on and another to let go, / A right time to rip out and another to mend, / A right time to shut up and another to speak up, / A right time to love and another to hate, / A right time to wage war and another to make peace." (Eccl 3:1–8, TM)

Sun(down, rise, set, shine, -ny)

JD: Many different Denver songs contain the word *sun*, sundown, sunrise, sunset, sunshine, or sunny. The most used word, *sunshine*, appears six times in the lyrics and once in the title of "Sunshine on My Shoulders" on the *PPP* album. Denver sings about sunshine on his shoulders making him happy; sunshine in his eyes makes him cry; sunshine on the waters looks lovely; and sunshine makes him high. He sings that his wish is for sunshine all the time, because sunshine almost always makes him high all the time.

The word *sun* helps to describe Zachary as shining laughter in the sun in "Zachary and Jennifer" on the *FA* album, while there are children raised beneath the golden sun in "I Want to Live" on the album with the same name. In "Eclipse" on the *BHA* album, he sings about thinking that sometimes he will never see the sun again, but also singing that the sun slowly fades in the western sky. His back is turned towards the sun in "Fire and Rain" on the *PPP* album. He is in Wyoming looking for the sun in "Whiskey Basin Blues" on the *FA* album, and seven days have passed and he hasn't seen the sun in "Wrangell Mountain Song" on the *AUTO* album. After looking around Denver sings that his eyes cannot find the sun in "To the Wild Country" on the *ES* album.

In "Boy from the Country" on the *AEJD* album, the listener learns that the boy from the country loves the sun, while Denver explains that he has learned how to listen for a sound like the sun going down in "Song for the Life" on the *AUTO* album, and daisies swayed by the wind sing a lazy song beneath the sun in "Mother Nature's Son" on the *RMH* album. The sun sinks behind him in the west in "A Little Further North" on *FTSS* album. No matter where a person is in the world, it is the same old sun in the sky in "Shanghai Breezes" on the *GH3* album. Denver rides off in the sun in "Baby, You Look Good to Me Tonight" on the *SP* album, while he sings about a race for the sun in "The Gold and Beyond" on the *GH3* album. While Alaska is the land of the midnight sun in "American Child" on the *AUTO* album, the shadows of the sun cover the graves in "Whalebones and Crosses" on the same album. In "Sticky Summer Weather" on the *TMT* album, he compares a dream he cannot recall to the sun hiding behind a cloud. He likes seeing a clear blue sky and a brightly shining sun in "Season Suite: Spring" on the *RMH* album.

In "Earth Day Every Day (Celebrate)" on the *ES* album, Denver defines evening as the time the stars appear in the loss of the sun. He promises to give his beloved all his sun days in "True Love Takes Time" on the *OW* album. In "Matthew" on the *BHA* album, he describes a Kansas farm boy riding on his father's shoulders behind a mule beneath the sun. Similarly, In "Catch Another Butterfly" on the *R&R* album, he has his own son in mind when he sings that the morning sun was there for rise and shine. In "Islands" on the *SH* album, the islands are described as being stepping stones to the sun. He urges listeners to look to the sun in "Joseph & Joe" on the *JD* album, while in "The Gift You Are" on *FTSS* album, he tells his beloved to make believe that the sun is her own lucky star.

Other than the use of sunshine, as indicated above in "Sunshine on My Shoulders," Denver uses three words for sun in "Season Suite: Summer" on the *RMH* album. He sings about the sun coming up, the promise of a sunny day, and the flowers that open to gather sunshine. In "Season Suite: Winter" on the same album, he states that it is more than worth waiting during the winter for another chance to see the summer sun. In "Back Home Again" on the same album, he recounts that someone's mother called a few days before to report that sunshine made her cry. In One World on the album with the same name, Denver sings that the day consists of flowers in the sunshine. He loves to see the sun go down in "Around and Around" on the *PPP* album, while in the light of the sunshine he can fly away in "On the Wings of An Eagle" on the *FJ* album. In "Relatively Speaking" on the *SH* album, he tells his unnamed beloved that he needs her like the sunshine needs the shadows and the night. In "Healing Time on Earth," an unrecorded song, Denver sings that the world awakens to the rising sun. Likewise, in "The Gift You Are" on *FTSS* album, he tells his beloved to imagine the moment when the sun comes shining through after a month of cloudy days; then, he asks her to imagine that she is that ray of sunshine. In "High Wind Blowin'" on the *FJ* album, he tells his beloved that she looks like the twilight falling on the ocean in the setting sun.

Denver sings about lazy, sunny days with nothing much to do in "Cool an' Green an' Shady" on the *BHA* album. In "I'd Rather Be a cowboy (Lady's Chains)" on the *FA* album, Denver is lying in the mountains and singing songs for sunny days. He's seen sunny days that he thought would never end in "Fire and Rain" on the *PPP* album.

While we have already encountered the sun rising above, in "Ponies" on the *DD* album, he tells the ponies that he wants to fly with them across the sunrise to see what begins each shining day. In "The Foxfire Suite: You

Are" on the *DD* album he tells an unidentified someone that he or she is every morning sunrise. In "Cowboy's Delight" on the *WIND* album, he sings songs of the sunrise into the night, and in "Shipmates and Cheyenne" on the same album, he holds out for just one rising sun. To someone recently born, Denver sings that he or she felt the urge of the sun's light beams when in the womb in "Ancient Rhymes" on *FTSS* album.

Finally, while we have experienced the setting sun, in "I'd Rather Be a Cowboy (Lady's Chains)" on the *FA* album, he sings about laughing with the rain and the sunshine and lying his sundown in some starry field. He states that he loves burning sundowns "In the Grand Way" on the *SP* album. Thus, Denver uses sun, sundown, sunrise, sunshine, and sunny not only to refer to the largest star in the Milky Way, but to convey emotions of joy, serenity, melancholy, and reflection, among others.

Scripture: "What do people gain from all the toil / at which they toil under the sun? / The sun rises and the sun goes down, / and hurries to the place where it rises. / What has been is what will be, / and what has been done is what will be done; / there is nothing new under the sun. / Is there a thing of which it is said, 'See, this is new'? / It has already been, / in the ages before us." (Eccl 1:3, 5, 9–10, NRSV)

Reflection: The HB (OT) book of Ecclesiastes, supposedly written by one called The Teacher, The Preacher, or Qoheleth, offers observations based on human experiences, just like Denver sings about his human experiences. After asking if there is any benefit from life during wearisome, earthly existence, the author concludes that nothing ever changes. Living life is a daily experience, just like the sun rising and the sun setting every day. In the biblical world—most likely borrowed from the Egyptian understanding—the setting sun goes under the flat-plate-like second level of the universe called the earth in the west to rise the next day again in the east. In other words, the sun is predicable, just like most human behavior is predictable. Nothing changes. In the words of Ecclesiastes, "All things are wearisome; / more than one can express" (Eccl 1:8a). While Denver's use of sun is usually positive, The Teacher's use of sun is usually negative, because it reflects the daily flow of human existence.

Meditation/Journal: For you does the sun represent what is positive or negative about human existence? Explain. Out of the uses of sun by Denver, which one is your favorite? Why?

Canticle Response: "Blessed are you, O Lord, God of our ancestors! You alone are praiseworthy and high above us, and your name will be blessed forever! / All creation, bless the Lord; praise and honor him forever. /

Everything above creation, bless the Lord; praise and honor him forever. / Sun and moon, bless the Lord; praise and honor him forever. (Dan 3:52, 57–58, 62 [Sg Three 1:29, 35–36, 40], TM)

Surrender

JD: Surrender, meaning to relinquish, yield, or relent, appears in two of Denver's songs. He is looking for something to believe in, something to do with his life in "Sweet Surrender" on the *BHA* album. He sings about tomorrow being open and not knowing the future, but the spirit is guiding him to live without care, which is sweet surrender. In "Hold on Tightly" on the *IAT* album, he sings about holding on tightly, letting go lightly, because it is only surrender. He doesn't use the word *surrender* in "Perhaps Love" on the *SH* album, but he refers to it when he sings that some people say that love is holding on, and other people say that love is letting go. While Denver embraces the uncertainties of life and finds peace in letting go, he also discusses the balance between holding on and letting go; for Denver surrender is an unknown part of life's journey.

Scripture: ". . . [T]he LORD said [to Cain], 'What have you done? Listen; your brother's [, Abel's,] blood is crying out to me from the ground! And now you are cursed from the ground, which has opened its mouth to receive your brother's blood from your hand. When you till the ground, it will no longer yield to you its strength; you will be a fugitive and a wanderer on the earth.'" (Gen 4:10–12, NRSV)

Reflection: While the English translation of the New Revised Standard Version Bible does not any where use the word *surrender*, it does use the word *yield* in the sense of surrender. Abel, a shepherd, and Cain, a farmer, bring their offerings from the flock and the farm, respectively, to the LORD. For no given reason, the LORD prefers Abel's offering of a sheep, because animal offerings will occupy a primary place in Israelite and Jewish history. After Cain kills Abel, the LORD curses Cain's work as a farmer. A curse cuts off a person from something. In this case, the earth Cain farms is cursed; the ground will no longer surrender its ability to produce vegetables. This curse is, of course, like the one the LORD God bestows on the man; he had to toil in the ground in order to grow food, and he had to contend with thorns and thistles in order to eat the plants of the field (Gen 3:17c–18a). In other words, hard work is ahead to grow crops in the soil, because it will not surrender to the man. By killing Abel, Cain pours his blood on the ground, which is why it is cursed. Blood, both animal and human, was considered sacred because it contained the essence of life; thus, the giver of life, the LORD, gets involved when any blood is spilled (Deut 12:23; Lev 17:10). Furthermore, the spiritual concept of surrender to the LORD's or God's will is a major theme—usually phrased as keeping his commandments and statutes—throughout biblical literature.

Meditation/Journal: To whom have you surrendered? Explain.

Psalm Response: "Clear my name, GOD; / I've kept an honest shop. / I've thrown in my lot with you, GOD, and / I'm not budging. / Examine me, GOD, from head to foot, / order your battery of tests. / Make sure I'm fit / inside and out / So I never lose / sight of your love, / But keep in step with you, / never missing a beat. / You know I've been aboveboard with you; / now be aboveboard with me. / I'm on the level with you, GOD; / I bless you every chance I get." (Ps 26:1–3, 11–12, TM)

T

Time

JD: Denver's use of the word *time* conveys the understanding that a suitable moment has been chosen for something to be done or to take place. This is found in "It's About Time" on the album with the same name. In that song, Denver uses the word *time* fourteen times—fifteen times if one counts the word *time* in the title. Denver sings that it is about time that people realize that they are together and not apart, that they come to realize that it is everyone or it is no one, that they recognize the changes occurring in the weather, and that they note other changes. It is also about time that people begin to see that the only home they have is earth, to face the fact that they cannot survive alone, that they need to listen to the wind's voice, and that they turn around the world, making it the dream they know and the peace they want. It is about time that all work together. In "On the Wings of a Dream" on the *IAT* album, he defines time as the moment at hand, the only thing we really know. Similarly, in "Today" on the *AEJD* album, he emphasizes that a certain today was his moment. In "Around and Around" on the *PPP* album, Denver sings that time as he has known it doesn't take much time to pass by. However, in "Wrangell Mountain Song" on the *AUTO* album, he sings that time passes slowly, when he is anxious about getting home; he also mentions that he gave time to serving his country. On the *WIND* album in "Shipmates and Cheyenne," he feels adrift in the meadow of time without a sense of progress, age, or direction. In "True Love Takes Time" on the *OW* album, he defines memories as the mysteries of time, but he also sings about how traveling takes time, and true love takes time, a phrase repeated nineteen times not counting the use of the word *time* in the title of the song. He states that he gives his listeners all the time it takes for them to understand. While his heart cannot say that he'll love a person till the end of time, he also cannot escape caring for the other person all the time in "I Can't Escape" on the *OW* album. His favorite time of day is sunset in "A Little Further North" on *FTSS* album; he also sings about losing track of time while fishing and remembering an easier time with silence, when the night sky is clear, further north. In "The Game Is Over" on the *FJ* album, he reminds his former beloved that there was a time when she could talk to him without speaking.

In two songs, Denver sings about healing time. In "Healing Time on Earth," an unrecorded song, he specifies healing time across the land, while walking with him on mother earth. And in "Love Is the Master" on the *OW* album, he tells everyone that time is the master of healing. For Denver, now, the present—as distinguished from the past or the future—is the moment or period when some actions need to take place.

Scripture: Esther sent a message to her uncle, Mordecai, saying, "'All the king's [Ahasuerus'] servants and the people of the king's [127] provinces know that if any man or woman goes to the king inside the inner court without being called, there is but one law—all alike are to be put to death. Only if the king holds out the golden scepter to someone, may that person live. I myself have not been called to come in to the king for thirty days.' When they told Mordecai what Esther had said, Mordecai told them to reply to Esther, 'Do not think that in the king's palace you will escape [death] any more than all the other Jews. For if you keep silence at such a time as this, relief and deliverance will rise for the Jews from another quarter, but you and your father's family will perish. Who knows? Perhaps you have come to royal dignity for just such a time as this.'" (Esth 4:11–14, NRSV)

Reflection: The author of the HB (OT) historical fiction book of Esther thinks that time is a suitable moment for something to take place. Esther, a Jewess, finds herself in the city of Susa, which three years previously had been a part of the Babylonian empire. Now a city of the Persian empire and one of three royal residences, King Ahasuerus, who rules 127 provinces, divorces his queen, who refuses to come when he calls her. He orders that young women be brought to his palace, and from them he will choose a new queen. Esther is among the young women, and she is chosen to be the king's new wife. The king also appoints a man named Haman to be next in command to himself. When Mordecai refuses to bow to Haman, Haman hatches a plot to get rid of all the Jews living in Ahasuerus' realm. After Esther tells him about Haman's plans, Mordecai urges her to approach the king and tell him what Haman is going to do. After she reminds Mordecai about the law of the land that no one can approach the king under penalty of death without the king's summons, Mordecai reminds his niece that she may have come to royal power—chosen as the kings wife—for such a time as this: Haman's plan to destroy all Jews in the empire. After prayer and fasting, Esther summons her courage, approaches her husband, tells him what Haman is planning to do to her people, watches as the king destroys Haman, and takes the king's ring to seal letters that will be sent to the Jews throughout the Persian empire informing the Jews that they will not be destroyed. In other words, Esther seizes this suitable moment and acts; she does not let much time pass by.

Meditation/Journal: In your life, identify one suitable moment that you used to bring about a change either in your life or in another's life. Explain how you came to realize that that moment at hand was the only thing you really owned.

Psalm Response: "Take the side of your servant, good God . . . . / I can't keep my eyes open any longer, waiting for you / to keep your promise to set everything right. / Let your love dictate how you deal with me; / teach me from your textbook on life. / I'm your servant—help me understand what that means, / the inner meaning of your instructions. / It's time to act, GOD; / they've made a shambles of your revelation!" (Ps 119:122a 123–126, TM)

Trees

JD: Denver uses the word *trees* in three different ways in his songs. First, he sings about trees in general. In "The Flower That Shattered the Stone" on the *ES* album, he defines the earth as a mother turning around with trees in the forest with their roots underground. In "Amazon" on the *DD* album, he states that in the forest there is a tree that represents all forests, and all trees are that one tree; later in the song he identifies it as the tree of temptation, an indirect reference to the tree of the knowledge of good and evil in the HB (OT) book of Genesis (2:9; 3:1–13). In the "Boy From the Country" on the *AEJD* album, he explains that the boy from the country does not want to see the forest for the trees. In "American Child" on the *AUTO* album, he sings about a promise made to the trees in Alaska. He sings about trees rushing by, when in an airplane in "Eli's Song" on the *SP* album. He sings about loving colored autumn trees in "In the Grand Way" on the *SP* album. There are no telephones in the trees, he sings, in "River" on the *FJ* album. In "Plant Conservation Trees" on the National Arbor Day Foundation PSA's album, he sings about planting a tree for tomorrow, one that clears the air, trees for America, a tree today for all the world to share. He urges listeners to plant a tree now and recognize all that the effort is worth: it is a place for birds to sing, a part of the forest for the future, and the breath of life.

Second, Denver gives specific names of trees in some songs. The most obvious in this category is aspen; it is obvious because his home was located near Aspen, Colorado, which got its name from the tree. In "Aspenglow" on the *TMT* album, not only does he use aspen, after which the city is named, but he explains that the song's title refers to the sense of family that shows in the citizens' lives and actions. However, in that song he also names the pine tree. He names the pine tree in "The Mountain Song" on the *AUTO* album. He mentions the aspen tree on the *AER* album in "Starwood in Aspen," a song about getting to his home, named Starwood, and in "The Harder They Fall" on the *DE* album, he begins on a Saturday night in Aspen, Colorado. There is something about a canyon in the shade of a cottonwood tree in "Something About" on the *IAT* album, there is an old pawpaw tree in "Nothing but a Breeze" on the *SH* album, and there are evergreens in "Johnny B. Goode" on the *JD* album.

Third, Denver mentions leaves that fall from deciduous trees. In "Whispering Jesse" on the *HG* album, he sings that he has always loved the green of new leaves in springtime. In "Cool an' Green an' Shady" on the *BHA* album, he has memories of aspen leaves trembling in the wind. In "Season Suite: Fall" on the *RMH* album, falling leaves whisper that winter is on the way. He sings that leaves will bow when his beloved walks by in "For Baby (For Bobbie)" on the *RMH* album, and he sings that his beloved is all the falling leaves in "The Foxfire Suite: You Are" on the *DD* album. In "Falling Leaves (The Refugees)" on the *HG* album, he sings that refugees are like falling leaves and asks that the falling leaves (refugees) be blessed.

Scripture: "Abram took his wife Sarai and his brother's son Lot, and all the possessions that they had gathered, and the persons whom they had acquired in Haran; and they set forth to go to the land of Canaan. Abram passed through the land to the place at Shechem, to the oak of Moreh. Then, the LORD appeared to Abram, and said, 'To your offspring I will give this land.' So he built there an altar to the LORD, who had appeared to him." (Gen 12:5–6a, 7, NRSV)

Reflection: Old biblical translations used to call the tree of Moreh a terebinth, until biblical scholars figured out that it was a big oak tree. Abram, later changed to Abraham (like Sarai later changed to Sarah), likes oak trees; after he and Lot separate, he moves his tent and "settled by the oaks of Mamre, which are at Hebron; and there he built an altar to the LORD" (Gen 13:18, NRSV). Later, the LORD "appeared to Abraham by the oaks of Mamre, as he sat at the entrance of his tent in the heat of the day" (Gen 18:1). What many biblical readers fail to notice is that a large oak tree is not only a sacred place—since Abra(ha)m builds altars to the LORD under them—but they connect the three stories of the universe. Until Copernicus and Galileo came along, ancient people—both Israelites and others—conceived of their universe as consisting of three levels, like a three-storied building. The first level, underground, named Sheol, is where the dead lived; the next level up is the flat, plate-like surface of the earth over which is stretched a dome and which is supported by seven pillars is where people live; and above the waters above the dome is heaven (or the heavens) where the LORD lives. A large oak tree has roots that reach deep underground which anchor its trunk on the earth, while its branches reach into the heavens. Thus, an oak tree is a conduit for the divine, the living, and the dead, who were often buried under oak trees. Denver's songs about trees and their leaves treat the woody plants with the sacredness they deserve biblically.

Meditation/Journal: What is your favorite tree? What does it represent for you? Explain.

Psalm Response: "What a beautiful thing, GOD, to give thanks, / to sing an anthem to you, the High God! / To announce your love each daybreak, / sing your faithful presence all through the night. / My ears are filled with the sounds of promise: / 'Good people will prosper like palm trees, / Grow tall like Lebanon cedars; / transplanted to GOD's courtyard, / They'll grow tall in the presence of God, / lithe and green, virile still in old age.'" (Ps 92:1–2, 12–14, NRSV)

U

Untrespassed

JD: Denver uses the word *untrespassed* in only one song: "Flight" on the *IAT* album. Not only did Denver know how to fly a plane, but he loved the experiences of flying, and he died in a plane crash. In the song he mentions flying through the wind-swept heights, and with silent, lifting mind passing the high untrespassed sanctity of space. He sings about putting out his hand and touching the face of God. *Untrespassed* is not a standard word; in other words, Denver created it—using poetic license—from *un*, meaning not, and *trespass*, meaning to go onto somebody else's land or enter someone's property without permission. Thus, *untrespassed* means *not trespassed, not infringed, not encroached upon*. The standard way of expressing *untrespassed* would be *not trespassed*, the opposite of *trespassed*.

Scripture: ". . . [T]he free gift [of God in Jesus Christ] is not like the trespass. For if the many died through the one man's trespass, much more surely have the grace of God and the free gift in the grace of the one man, Jesus Christ, abounded for the many. And the free gift is not like the effect of the one man's sin. For the judgment following one trespass brought condemnation, but the free gift following many trespasses brings justification. If, because of the one man's trespass, death exercised dominion through that one, much more surely will those who receive the abundance of grace and the free gift of righteousness exercise dominion in life through the one man, Jesus Christ. Therefore just as one man's trespass led to condemnation for all, so one man's act of righteousness leads to justification and life for all." (Rom 5:15–18, NRSV)

Reflection: According to Paul in his letter to the Romans, universal death entered the human race through the trespass of Adam (Gen 3:1–19), who, for Paul, is a type—a figure with important similarities—of Jesus Anointed, God's free gift. Just as Adam's action of eating fruit from the tree of the knowledge of good and evil brought universal death, God's action in Jesus brought universal justification (the righting of people's relationship with God) and righteousness (the renewed state of people's relationship with God). God's grace—God's gift of himself—overwhelmed the trespass and restored people to the state, in Denver's word, of being untrespassed and ready to receive eternal life.

Meditation/Journal: What aspect(s) of your life remain untrespassed? Explain.

Prayer Response: "Our Father, who art in heaven, / hallowed be thy name; / thy kingdom come, / thy will be done / on earth as it is in heaven. / Give us this day our daily bread, / and forgive us our trespasses, / as we forgive those who trespass against us; / and lead us not into temptation, but deliver us from evil." ("The Order of Mass" in *The Roman Missal*, par. 124)

V

Vision

JD: Denver uses the word *vision* to present a soaring image of freedom and harmony with nature in "Eagles and Horses" on *FTSS* album. He sings about having a vision of eagles and horses racing the wind and climbing higher and higher, like he did when flying. He compares the speed of eagles and horses to his spirit, which cannot be broken or caught because it flies freely.

Denver also uses the word *vision* to refer to an inner calling toward a personal aspiration in pursuit of his dreams. In "Higher Ground" on the album with the same name, he sings about living up to the vision, otherwise referred to as the dream in him and the commitment to follow his heart until it brings him home. In "A Wild Heart Looking for Home" on the *DE* album, he thinks of his beloved's face again, which he calls a vision to have and to hold, while spending a night all alone. Likewise, in "Let Us Begin" on the *OW* album, he urges his listeners to commit themselves to begin the process of peace, if peace is their vision. On the *JD* album in "Joseph & Joe," he sings about Joseph's vision being greater than his. In other words, the ability to anticipate the possible future or development is greater for Joseph than it is for Denver.

In "Children of the Universe" on the *SH* album, the vision has a heritage that life is more than always choosing sides. Denver's insight is that the broader view of life presents a collective understanding of humanity and nature. Such things as the rose's smell, the bird's song, and moonlight are given to everyone to enjoy and not just to a few. According to Denver in "Amazon" on the *DD* album, there is a collective vision that shines in the darkness, and that one vision comprises all human dreams. All human dreams are that one vision, which is a vision of heaven, according to Denver. In "The Gift You Are" on *FTSS* album, he sings that his beloved is the vision of prophets and sages, and that she is the only one. Thus, for Denver, the word *vision* conveys themes of inspiration, personal growth, and a deep connection with nature that is shared by all people, all children of the world.

Scripture: ". . . [T]here was a disciple in Damascus named Ananias. The Lord said to him in a vision, 'Ananias.' He answered, 'Here I am, Lord.' The Lord said to him, 'Get up and go to the street called Straight, and at the house of Judas look for a man of Tarsus named Saul. At this moment he is praying, and he has seen in a vision a man named Ananias come in and lay his hands on him so that he might regain his sight.' So Ananias went and entered the house. He laid his hands on Saul and said, 'Brother Saul, the Lord Jesus, who appeared to you on your way here, has sent me so that you may regain your sight and be filled with the Holy Spirit.' And immediately something like scales fell from his eyes, and his sight was restored." (Acts 9:10–12, 17–18, NRSV)

Reflection: The above passage from the CB (NT) Acts of the Apostles— the second volume of Luke's Gospel written by the same author—presents a vision about a vision. Saul (Paul) on his way to Damascus experienced light and voices, then he fell to the ground; when he got up, he was blind. According to the author, Ananias, a disciple, also hears a voice and goes to Saul (Paul), who has been blind for three days. The Lord, Jesus, tells him where to find Saul (Paul), to lay his hands on his head—the sign of giving the Holy Spirit—and heal him. Ananias does what the vision tells him and then baptizes Saul (Paul). The author of the Acts of the Apostles presumes that the inner calling received by both Saul (Paul) and Ananias comes from the Lord Jesus, who was crucified, died, buried, and raised from the dead. According to the author of the Acts of the Apostles, Ananias' vision enables Saul's (Paul's) mission to begin of proclaiming Jesus as the Son of God (Acts 9:20).

Meditation/Journal: What is your vision of your life and its mission? Explain.

Psalm Response: GOD, "A long time ago you spoke in a vision, / you spoke to your faithful beloved: / 'I've crowned a hero, / I chose the best I could find; / I found David, my servant, / poured holy oil on his head, / And I'll keep my hand steadily on him, / yes, I'll stick with him through thick and thin. / I'll preserve him eternally in my love, / I'll faithfully do all I so solemnly promised.'" (Ps 89:19–20, 33–34, TM)

Vow

JD: There is only one John Denver song that uses the word *vow*. "Let Us Begin" on the *OW* album, uses the word *vow* two times. Denver asks if people have forgotten all the vows that were taken when saying never again to war and weapons. He also asks if listeners have forgotten all the vows that were taken when saying never again to lives given to wars. Because a vow is a serious promise to perform a certain act, to carry out an activity, or to behave in a specific manner, Denver uses the word *promise* in a manner like his use of vow in "My Sweet Lady" on the *PPP* album. He promises his lady that he will stay beside her. Then, hinting at marriage vows, he sings about their lives being joined and entwined. In "Poems, Prayers and Promises" on the album with the same name, he sings about lying by the fire and talking about poems, prayers, and promises and other things believed in. Another hint that the word *vow* is in the back of his mind is found in "Autograph" on the album with the same name. Denver sings about always being with the person he loves and she being always with him. Thus, a serious promise, spoken or understood, is a vow.

Scripture: "The LORD spoke to Moses, saying: Speak to the Israelites and say to them: When either men or women make a special vow, the vow of a Nazirite, to separate themselves to the LORD, they shall separate themselves from wine and strong drink; they shall drink no wine vinegar or other vinegar, and shall not drink any grape juice or eat grapes, fresh or dried. All their days as nazirites they shall eat nothing that is produced by the grapevine, not even the seeds or the skins. All the days of their Nazirite vow no razor shall come upon the head; until the time is completed for which they separate themselves to the LORD, they shall be holy; they shall let the locks of the head grow long." (Num 6:1–5, NRSV)

Reflection: While many biblical readers have never heard of nazirites, they existed among the Israelites. Men and women could take vows to offer themselves for special service to the LORD for a specific time. Samson (Judg 13:2–14) and Samuel (1 Sam 1:11) are examples of nazirites. Besides abstaining from wine, vinegar, and other grape products and refraining from cutting the hair, nazirites were careful not to become ritually impure by contact with a corpse or a grave. Usually, the nazirite vow was for a designated time, but there were people who made the vow for the duration of their lives. Nazirite comes from the Hebrew word *nazir* meaning *consecrated* or *separated*. It is derived from a root word meaning *vow*. The word *nazir* is also the root for Nazareth, Jesus' hometown (Mark 1:9, 24; 10:47; 16:6; Matt 2:23; 26:71; Luke 1:26; 4:16, 34; 18:5, 7, 37; 19:1924:19; John 1:46; 19:19; Acts 2:22; 6:14; 10:38; 22:8; 26:9), especially the note in Matthew's Gospel that he was to be called a Nazorean (Matt 2:23). As Denver notes using the word *vow*, most people understand it to refer to marriage promises.

Meditation/Journal: What vows (promises) have you ever made? To whom did you make the vow? Of what did it consist? Explain.

Psalm Response: "What can I give back to GOD / for the blessings he's poured out on me? / I'll lift high the cup of salvation—a toast to GOD! / I'll pray in the name of GOD; / I'll complete what I promised GOD I'd do . . . . / Oh GOD, here I am, your servant, / your faithful servant: set me free for your service! / I'm ready to offer the thanksgiving sacrifice / and pray in the name of GOD. / I'll complete what I promised GOD I'd do . . . ." (Ps 116:12–14a, 16–18a, TM)

W

Wind

JD: The word *wind* is the most used word in songs by Denver. In "Windsong" on the album with the same name, Denver presents the characteristics of the wind, some of which are echoed in other songs. The wind, according to Denver, is the whisper of mother earth, the hand of father sky, the watcher of struggles and pleasures, the goddess who learned to fly, the bearer of good and bad tidings, the weaver of darkness, the bringer of dawn, the giver of rain, the builder of rainbows, the singer of the first song, a twister of anger and warning, the bringer of the fragrance of freshly mowed hay, a racer—like a wild stallion running, the sweet taste of love on a slow summer day, the knower of songs of the cities and canyons; the thunderer of mountains, the roarer of the sea, the taker and giver of morning, and the symbol of all that is free. After naming all those characteristics, Denver tells his listeners to welcome the wind and to sing with the wind.

Singing with the wind involves listening to the sounds of the wind. In "Spirit" on the *WIND* album, Denver sings about loving the wind and learning her song. In "Dancing with the Mountains" on the *AUTO* album, he sings that all are one when singing in the wind. For Denver the usual word to describe the sound of the wind is whisper. In "The Foxfire Suite: Whisper the Wind" on the *DD* album, he says that the wind whispers over water, through the night, along canyons, and into the light; the wind whispers that all are brothers and sisters, all the same, and they should love one another; the wind also whispers names. Indeed, the wind whispers another's name to him in "For Baby (For Bobbie)" on the *RMH* album. In "Southwind" on the *JD* album, he sings about chasing the shouting winds aloft. One can hear a tune in the wind, Denver says, in "The Ballad of St. Anne's Reel" on the *AUTO* album; when the wind is right, there is a melody. In "The Flower That Shattered the Stone" on the *ES* album, Denver identifies the wind as the sigh of the father above. As such, the wind has the power to shut an open door, while still being gentle and loving like the songbird in "A Wild

Heart Looking for Home" on the *DE* album. In "Love Is Everywhere" on the *WIND* album, Denver sings about the sound of the wind singing dreams for him.

The wind is free as a wind-swell in "Calypso" on the *WIND* album, while in "Eagles and Horses" on *FTSS* album, eagles and horses race the wind. In "Wild Montana Skies" on the *IAT* album, Denver sings about giving the wild wind as a brother to the Montana child. The strongness of the wind is emphasized in "Season Suite: Fall" on the *RMH* album, when Denver reflects that it is a shame to see the month of September swallowed by the wind. Similarly, in "High Wind Blowin'" on the *FJ* album, he sings that there is such a high wind blowing that it was snowing on his bed, and that he would not get the sleep that night because of the wind's noise. He sings about topping the wind-swept heights with easy grace in "Flight (The Higher We Fly)" on the *IAT* album. In "Whalebones and Crosses" on the *AUTO* album, Denver sings about the wind blowing through the graveyard where ancestors lie buried. The strength of the wind is highlighted in "Four Strong Winds" on the *FJ* album; Denver sings that they blow lonely. The wind was made for kites in "Catch Another Butterfly" on the *R&R* album, while the old "Hitchhiker" on the *SP* album held his thumb in it to get a ride; that action was better than crying in the wind. In "Pegasus" on the *SP* album, Denver sings about the man who saddled the wind. The allusion is to a 1958 film, *Saddle the Wind*, which uses the metaphorical idea of attempting to control or subdue something that is inherently untamed or uncontrollable, like the wind. In the film, a troubled character with a gun needs to be tamed by his older brothers.

In Denver's songs, the wind can come from any direction. In "Wild Montana Skies" on the *IAT* album, Denver mentions wild geese who bring a warm wind from the south. Likewise, in "Southwind" on the *JD* album, he says that a south wind blows his love to his beloved. There are several songs about cold winds; one can feel snow in the chill of the wind in "Love Is the Master" on the *OW* album; in the spring the wind is cool and clean in "Sticky Summer Weather" on the *TMT* album; in "Four Strong Winds" on the *FJ* album, the four winds can blow cold, and when a cold wind blows, it can turn your head around in "Fire and Rain" on the *PPP* album. However, a warm wind feels alright in "High Wind Blowin'" on the *FJ* album.

In "Dancing with the Mountains" on the *AUTO* album, Denver says that he dances in the wind. That is why in "The Eagle and the Hawk" on the *AER* album, he invites his listeners to come dance with the west wind. He sings about dreaming that he was a mountain in the wind in "The Wings That Fly Us Home" on the *SP* album. He is one with the wind in "On the Wings of an Eagle" on the *FJ* album. He compares the revolving thoughts of an old man to the wind in "Shipmates and Cheyenne" on the *WIND* album. He says to go tell that the battle is over and the war is done to those with the wind in their noses, because they fall like weeds in the wind during war in "You Say the Battle is Over" on the *AUTO* album. In "Rusty Green" on the *FJ* album, he sees winds clouding the sun.

While a breeze is not a wind, it is mentioned often in Denver's songs. Softly, like a baby's breath, a breeze begins to whisper, sings Denver in "Season Suite: Summer" on the *RMH* album, while in "Season Suite: Spring" on the same album, he says that one can hear the breezes say that everything that was cold and gray of winter is gone. In "Song for the Life" on the *AUTO* album, the midsummer days flow like a breeze through one's mind, which is why in "Windsong" on the album with the same name he urges his listeners in heart and spirit to let the breezes surround them. In "Nothing but a Breeze" on *SH* album, he sings that people do as they please, because it isn't anything but a breeze. In "Shanghai Breezes" on the *GH3* album, he says that the voice he hears in his ears is like heaven to him and like the breezes in Shanghai. He urges listeners to open their ears and hear the breeze's song about the cold and gray of winter being gone in "Season Suite: Spring" on the *RMH* album, while breezes murmur in "A Little Further North" on *FTSS* album. Thus, while wind can be wild and free, a breeze is tamed and gentle.

Scripture: ". . . [E]very matter has its time and way, although the troubles of mortals lie heavy upon them. Indeed, they do not know what is to be, for who can tell them how it will be? No one has power over the wind to restrain the wind, or power over the day of death . . . . All this I [, the Teacher,] observed, applying my mind to all that is done under the sun . . . ." (Eccl 8:6–8a, 9a, NRSV)

Reflection: In the biblical world, like in the Denver world, the wind cannot be harnessed; it is free. It can be used for transportation on the ocean or sea, it can be employed to winnow grain, and it is a potent force of nature on both land and sea. It was harnessed between 500 and 900 CE in Persia, where windmills were designed to pump water and grind grain. By the 1800s CE it was used to generate electricity, a process continuing to be refined into modern times. Thus, when the Teacher in the above passage reflects that no one has the power to harness or restrain the wind, he is correct for his time and place. Likewise, no one could know the future, especially the day of death, just like no one could exercise power over the wild wind. Denver echoes these understandings in his various songs about the wind. Biblically, it is important to note here that the Hebrew word *ruah* and Greek word *pneuma* can be translated into English as wind, spirit, or breath. Thus it is just as accurate to translate the sentence from the above biblical passage as no one has power over the breath (or spirit), as it is to translate it as no one has power over the wind. Using the two alternate English words, adds a depth of meaning to the phrase.

Meditation/Journal: What English words are derived from the Greek word *pneuma*? Make a list. After each word indicate whether it refers to wind, breath, or spirit.

Psalm Response: "GOD, my God, how great you are! / beautifully, gloriously robed, / Dressed up in sunshine, / and all heaven stretched out for your tent. / You built your palace on the ocean deeps, / made a chariot out of clouds and took off on wind-wings. / You commanded winds as messengers, / appointed fire and flame as ambassadors. / You set earth on a firm foundation / so that nothing can shake it, ever." (Ps 104:1b–5, TM)

Winter

JD: Other than using the word *winter* in two subtitles of "Season Suite," namely "Winter" and "Late Winter, Early Spring (When Everybody Goes to Mexico)" on the *RMH* album, Denver expresses a positive-negative feeling about winter. His positivity is found in "Aspenglow" on the *TMT* album. He sings about tasting the warmth of winter wine and that as the days of winter unfold, the hearts of those in Aspen, Colorado, grow warmer with the cold. Also, repeatedly, he sings about winter skol (cheers). Ironically, on the same album is found "Sticky Summer Weather," in which Denver sings about not being able to stand the thought of winter! Further negativity concerning the winter season is associated with sadness and the coming of winter in "Rhymes and Reasons" on the album with the same name. In "Whispering Jesse" on the *HG* album, he expresses his love for springtime, which he clarifies by singing about the passing of winter. He states he cannot live on the promises of winter to spring in "Today" on the *AEJD* album. In "Whiskey Basin Blues" on the *FA* album, he says that there is a reason no one else can see—a lady in Laramie, Wyoming—for a good man to spend the winter on his own in an old cabin. In "Wrangell Mountain Song" on the *SP* album, Denver sings about it being colder and winter being in the air. And in "Two Shots" on the *WIND* album, he mentions speaking about a cold winter's morning. Thus, Denver leans more negatively toward the season of winter than he does positively.

Scripture: ". . . Noah built an altar to the LORD, and took of every clean animal and of every clean bird, and offered burnt offerings on the altar. And when the LORD smelled the pleasing odor, the LORD said in his heart, 'I will never again curse the ground because of humankind, for the inclination of the human heart is evil from youth; nor will I ever again destroy every living creature as I have done. As long as the earth endures, / seedtime and harvest, cold and heat, / summer and winter, day and night, / shall not cease.'" (Gen 8:20–22, NRSV)

Reflection: There are two different versions of the great flood story in the HB (OT) book of Genesis; the two versions—Yahwist and Priestly—have been woven into one to present a unified story. Some Bibles present a chart indicating from where various verses come from each account. The passage above is from the older version of the story, the Yahwist; it illustrates the Yahwist author's concerns. It is called the Yahwist version because it identifies God as Yahweh, presented in most Bibles as LORD. Another concern of the Yahwist is the building of an altar; the altar, usually made of stone, claims the territory for God; in other words, it identifies that a God-worshipper and his God is in the area! The Yahwist is also concerned about offering God only clean animals; this does not mean that they are physically without dirt. It means that they did not cross over perceived fix boundaries. Because this concept is foreign to many cultures, think of the unclean pig, which does not chew its cud and has split hooves; this makes it unlike clean animals, such as cows, sheep, and deer. The Yahwist writer will show more of his concern for altars and clean burnt offerings throughout the rest of the book of Genesis. The purpose of burnt offerings is to make invisible the visible cow, sheep, or deer so that it can be received and smelled by the invisible LORD. The Yahwist, who wrote the account of the fall of Eve and Adam (Gen 3:1–24), has a negative view of humankind, who tends toward evil. Nevertheless, he presents the LORD as being compassionate by pledging never again to destroy every living creature. The LORD promises not to disrupt—not revert to chaos (like the flood)—his created order of seasons (summer and winter; heat and cold), agricultural rhythms (seedtime and harvest), and daily rhythms (day and night). In other words, the chaos of the flood has resulted in the LORD recreating the order of the universe. Similarly, Denver's negative view of the chaos of winter ultimately culminates in the order of springtime.

Meditation/Journal: For you, what does winter represent? Explain.

Psalm Response: "God is my King from the very start; / he works salvation in the womb of the earth. / With one blow you split the sea in two . . . . / With your finger you opened up springs and creeks, / and dried up the wild floodwaters. / You own the day, you own the night; / you put stars and sun in place. / You laid out the four corners of earth, / shaped the seasons of summer and winter." (Ps 74:12–13a, 15–17, TM)

Wisdom

JD: Wisdom is the knowledge and experience needed to make sensible decisions and judgments, or it is the good sense shown by the decisions and knowledge. While he doesn't use the word *wisdom* as often as he uses other words in songs, nevertheless, Denver uses it in a few songs. In "Rhymes and Reasons" on the album with the same name, he urges listeners to seek the wisdom of the children and the graceful way of flowers bending in the wind. In other words, Denver appreciates the insight found in youth and in nature. In a similar way in "Healing Time on Earth," an unreleased song, Denver sings about listening to the mountains talk and the rivers run because there is a wisdom there, and there is much to learn from nature. Wisdom is not underground, he sings in "Come and Let Me Look in Your Eyes" on the *SP* album. In "Two Shots" on the *WIND* album, Denver sets the story in a bar, where, after speaking, others listened, as he spoke again, for the wisdom of what he might say. And in "Let It Be," a song written by Paul McCartney of The Beatles but on Denver's *PPP* album, he sings about unidentified Mother Mary speaking words of wisdom and whispering words of wisdom: let it be.

Scripture: ". . . I prayed, and understanding was given me; / I called on God, and the spirit of wisdom came to me. / May God grant me to speak with judgment, / and to have thoughts worthy of what I have received; / for he is the guide even of wisdom / and the corrector of the wise. / For it is he who gave me unerring knowledge of what exists, / to know the structure of the world and the activity of the elements; / the beginning and end and middle of times, / the alternations of the solstices and the changes of the seasons . . . . / I learned both what is secret and what is manifest, / for wisdom, the fashioner of all things, taught me."(Wis 7:7, 15, 17–18, 21–22, NRSV)

Reflection: There is a type of writing in the Bible known as wisdom literature. It includes the HB (OT) books of Job, Psalms, Proverbs, Ecclesiastes, and OT (A) books of Wisdom and Sirach. Such religious writing presents accumulated knowledge of life and the resulting behavior that results from experiences of God. Wisdom is often personified, as in Proverbs (1:20–33; 8:1–36). In the above passage, the speaker is King Solomon, who, in biblical literature, is known for his wisdom. Thus, in the OT (A) book of Wisdom, he speaks autobiographically (Wis 7:1—9:18). After praying, God gave him understanding and the spirit of wisdom. Then, he prayed for judgment, so that God would guide the wisdom he had bestowed on him. Wisdom also involves knowledge of many different things. According to Solomon, he learned both secret and obvious information, because wisdom, who fashioned all things (Prov 8:22–23, 30), taught him. Denver, in his songs, seeks both knowledge and experience of nature in order to be wise and to teach others to be wise.

Psalm Response: "What a wildly wonderful world, GOD! / You made it all, with Wisdom at your side, / made earth overflow with your wonderful creations. / All the creatures look expectantly to you / to give them their meals on time. / You come, and they gather around; / you open your hand and they eat from it. / If you turned your back, / they'd die in a minute— / Take back your Spirit and they die, / revert to original mud; / Send out your Spirit and they spring to life— / the whole countryside in bloom and blossom." (Ps 104:24, 27–30, TM)

X

eXperience

JD: Denver never used a word beginning with X in any song! And the word above—*experience*—does not begin with X, but it describes how important personal experience was to him in writing songs. The English word *experience* is a composition of three Latin parts. The first part is *ex*, meaning *out of* or *from*; the second part is *per*, meaning to *try* or to *risk*; and the third part is *ience*, from the Latin word *itus*, meaning *to go* or *to proceed*. When the last two parts of the Latin word are put together, they form *peritus*, meaning *expert* or *skilled*. After evolving from Latin through French to *esperience*, in Middle English it became experience. Thus, we have the English word *experience*, which means to go and take from the risk something that enriches one's life. Denver takes the process one step further; he reflects or contemplates the experience to get to a deeper insight about himself or the event and write songs about it. In "Whispering Jesse" on the *HG* album, he sings about wondering in deep contemplation evaluating various scenarios, the *coulds* and *shoulds,* and what he would do differently if he had the opportunity to do them again.

In "Looking for Space" on the *WIND* album, he sings about being on the road of experience in an effort to figure out who he was. He was looking for space, he sang, to find out who he was and both to know and to understand that it was a sweet dream. Having a healthy understanding of self is important in order to interpret experiences. Experiences are the basis of John Denver song lyrics in which he narrates travel within his home state of Colorado, in Wyoming, Alaska, Canada, and elsewhere. In songs about his relationships, he explores the meaning of the experience of relating to another human being. After reflecting upon his experiences, Denver wrote songs about them, surfacing information about the place where the experience occurred and presenting his insights about it. Such is the case with "Whispering Jesse" above. He explains how he wondered in deep contemplation, when alone, thinking about experiences. Denver's life consisted of one experience after another, the reflection on those experiences, and the writing of lyrics and music. In other words, his life was a road trip of experiences, and his life was spent interpreting and assigning meaning to them in order to look into them deeper and deeper.

That was Denver's process of spirituality; it was the way he lived his life and reflected on the experiences of it, especially love, the mountains, wind, etc. Sometimes moving, sometimes standing still, he wanted to find out who he was and what the experience made him to be. The process was a struggle, because he was always in the process of coming to be or change. This free-as-an-eagle man or deep in despair at being all-alone-in-the-universe man never stopped exploring. While recognizing how things and people are, he kept searching for the spirit under the experience.

Scripture: "If you gathered nothing in your youth, / how can you find anything in your old age? / How attractive is sound judgment in the gray-haired, / and for the aged to possess good counsel? / How attractive is wisdom in the aged, / and understanding and counsel in the venerable! / Rich experience is the crown of the aged, / and their boast is the fear of the Lord." (Sir 25:3–6, NRSV)

Reflection: Failure to reflect and contemplate during the days of youth mean that one will have gathered little or no wisdom for the older years. Throughout biblical literature and found in many cultures is respect for the opinion or perspective of those wearing gray hair. Giving good advice is also a biblical and cultural function of the aged. Those aged who have done the work of reflecting on experiences possess a treasure box full of wisdom. They understand why things are the way they are and, venerably, can share the results of their contemplation on their experiences with others. Because their experiences are rich, they are like a crown for the aged. Their boast is the fear—awesomeness—of the Lord; their boast is not themselves, but the one from whom all wisdom comes.

Meditation/Journal: What process do you use to mine your experiences: journaling, meditation, contemplating, talking to a friend, walking, etc.? What are the steps in your process to reach a deeper understanding or insight about experiences?

Psalm Response: "Hallelujah! / Sing to GOD a brand-new song, / praise him in the company of all who love him. / Let['s] . . . celebrate [our] Sovereign Creator, / . . . [let's] exult in [our] King. / Let['s] . . . praise his name in dance; / strike up the band and make great music! / And why? Because GOD delights in his people, / festoons plain folk with salvation garlands! (Ps 149:1–4, TM)

Y

You

JD: The word *you* is the second person pronoun for both the singular and the plural. In English, without knowing the antecedent noun one cannot tell if you is singular (one person) or plural (two or more people). Other languages present different words for the singular and plural you. For example, in Latin, the singular you is *tu*, while the plural you is *vos*; in French, the singular you is *tu*, and the plural you is *vous*; in Spanish, the singular you is *tu* or *usted*, and the plural you is *vosatros* or *vosatras* or *ustedes*. In English, the pronoun *you*—either singular or plural—requires an antecedent noun to identify who you is or who you are! Denver ignores that requirement in many songs by simply beginning the lyrics with you. Songs that have a proper name in the title, like "Annie's Song" on the BHA album, begins with *you*, and the listener concludes that *you's* antecedent noun is Annie in the title and must be the singular form of the pronoun. "Eli's Song" on the *SP* album, has no *you* until the second line. It leaves one wondering if the *you's* antecedent noun is Eli in the title or some other *you*, as can be found in many Denver songs.

In "Thought of You" on the *IAT* album, *you*, which has no antecedent noun in the title of the song, doesn't appear until the second stanza of the song and is used over ten times thereafter; however, no antecedent noun ever appears in the song to tell the listener who *you is* or who *you are*! The same scenario occurs in "The Gift You Are" on *FTSS* album; "Thanks to You" on the same album; "I Remember You" on the *OW* album; "The Foxfire Suite: You Are" on the *DD* album; "For You (Fifty Shades Freed)" on the *HG* album; "Farewell Andromeda" on the album with the same name; "This Old Guitar" on the *BHA* album; and "The Music Is You" on the same album.

This is but a sample of the many songs that contain the word *you* with no antecedent noun; there are many more songs that follow the same pattern.

Scripture: "You shall count off seven weeks of years, seven times seven years; so that this period of seven weeks of years gives forty-nine years. Then you shall have the trumpet sounded loud; on the tenth day of the seventh month—on the day of atonement—you shall have the trumpet sounded throughout all your land. And you shall hallow the fiftieth year and you shall proclaim liberty throughout the land to all its inhabitants. It shall be a jubilee for you: you shall return every one of you, to your property and every one of you to your family. That fiftieth year shall be a jubilee for you: you shall not sow, or reap the aftergrowth, or harvest the unpruned vines. For it is a jubilee; it shall be holy to you: you shall eat only what the field itself produces." (Lev 25:8–12, NRSV)

Reflection: In the biblical passage above from the HB (OT) book of Leviticus, no antecedent noun is provided. Someone opens a Bible and begins to read a passage that begins with *you*, as does the above passage. Who is or who are *you*? Is *you* singular or plural? There is no way to know unless the reader skims backward—before where he or she began—to find the antecedent noun. In some biblical books, the antecedent noun may be located two or more chapters before the passage read. In the passage above, the antecedent noun is found seven verses before. In Leviticus 25:1, "The LORD spoke to Moses on Mount Sinai, saying: Speak to the people of Israel and say to them:" (Lev 25:1–2a, NRSV). However, even that verse presents ambiguity, as to the antecedent noun: Is Moses the *you*, or Are the Israelites *you*? The reader, either consciously or unconsciously, must decide, but he or she needs the additional information even to begin to determine who *you* is or who *you* are!

In its context, the passage present the LORD inaugurating the jubilee year every fiftieth year. According to Leviticus, people were to return to their property and their family; this directive presumes that people return to the original allocation of the plots of land assigned to each Israelite tribe, clan, and family. However, the allocation was not narrated biblically until the HB (OT) book of Joshua (13—22). In other words, the authors of Leviticus are getting ahead of their own historical story! In ancient Israel, land may be sold and bought, but, because all land belongs to God, on the fiftieth year it reverts to the original owner. The sale and buying of land is, thus, temporary. Furthermore, the phrase, "proclaim liberty throughout the land" (Lev 25:10a) can be found inscribed on the Liberty Bell in Philadelphia; it was put there to represent the freedom and equality of all people in the United States. The bell was cast in 1752 in London after it was commissioned by the

Pennsylvania Assembly for the Pennsylvania State House (Independence Hall), but it cracked shortly after its arrival. It was recast from the same metal in 1753 by John Pass and John Stow in Philadelphia, and it cracked, too. Later in U.S. history, the phrase was applied to the abolition of slavery and the Civil Rights Movement. In other words, the original phrase addressed to Moses and the Israelites, which referred to proclaiming liberty, giving the land a rest, and returning to one's original plot was repurposed by the people of Philadelphia and then by the people of the U.S.

Meditation/Journal: In everyday life, where are you (singular) conscious of the word *you* being used in conversations, TV shows, and advertisements with no antecedent noun?

Psalm Response: "Count yourself lucky, how happy you must be— / you get a fresh start, / your slate's wiped clean. / Count yourself lucky— / GOD holds nothing against you / and you're holding nothing back from him. / Let me give you some good advice; / I'm looking you in the eye / and giving it to you straight: / 'Don't be ornery like a horse or mule / that needs bit and bridle / to stay on track.' / God-defiers are always in trouble; / GOD-affirmers find themselves loved / every time they turn around." (Ps 32:1–2, 8–10, TM)

Z

Zachary

JD: Zachary is the name of Denver's African-American adopted son—Zachary John Denver—while Denver was still married to Annie Martel. The name *Zachary* in English vernacular is derived from the biblical name *Zechariah*, meaning *the LORD remembers*. Denver mentions Zachary in two songs. In "Zachary and Jennifer" on the *FA* album, he sings about naming the baby Zachary and raising him in the mountains. He sings that he will bathe in crystal fountains, and he will be shining laughter in the sun. In "A Baby Just Like You" on the *ACT* album, he wishes little Zachary a Merry Christmas. Denver and Martel also adopted a little girl named Anna Kate Denver. After his divorce from Martel, he married Cassandra Delaney, who gave birth to Jesse Belle Deutschendorf.

Scripture: "In the eighth month, in the second year of Darius, the word of the LORD came to the prophet Zechariah son of Berechiah son of Iddo, saying: Thus says the LORD of hosts: Return to me, says the LORD of hosts, and I will return to you, says the LORD of hosts." (Zech 1:1, 3, NRSV)

Reflection: In biblical literature, there are twenty-seven men named Zechariah. Three are of particular importance. The first is the son of Jeroboam II, King of Israel; that Zechariah served as King of Israel for six months (2 Kgs 15:8–12). The second man to have the name *Zechariah* is the minor prophet, from whose book the above scripture passage is taken. The prophet Zechariah addressed the Jews who had returned from Babylon to Jerusalem by the order of King Cyrus of Persia under the kingship of his successor (522–486 BCE), Darius, in 520 BCE. Zechariah addressed the Jews who had returned to the ruins of Jerusalem and its Temple, encouraging them not to lose hope that God was in charge of history and that he had planned to restore Jerusalem and the Temple. Zechariah wrote to urge the returnees to get busy with the concrete process of rebuilding. In the above passage, Zechariah records the LORD telling him to tell his people that if they return both to Jerusalem and to God, that the LORD would return both to Jerusalem and to them. The sign of God's return was the rebuilding of the Temple (Ezra 5:1; 6:14). The third important Zechariah is found only in the CB (NT) gospel according to Luke. That Zechariah is a priest (Luke 1:5), who receives a revelation in the Temple that, despite their elder years, he and his wife, Elizabeth, would conceive and give birth to a son, who would be named John the Baptist (Luke 1:5–25, 57–80).

Meditation/Journal: Make a list of the men you know who are named Zechariah, Zachariah, Zacharias, Zachary, Zach, etc.

Psalm Response: "You walked off and left us, and never looked back. / God, how could you do that? / We're your very own sheep; / how can you stomp off in anger? / Refresh your memory of us—you bought us a long time ago. / Your most precious tribe—you paid a good price for us! / Your very own Mount Zion—you actually lived here once! / Come and visit the site of disaster, / see how they've wrecked the sanctuary. / Mark and remember, GOD .... / Remember your promises ...." (Ps 74:1–3, 18a, 20a, TM)

CONCLUSION

With the thirtieth anniversary of John Denver's death on October 12, 2027, we remember his spirituality as found in the lyrics of his songs. Through the lyrics of his songs and the music he wrote, he shares how his spirit inspired him to live his life of experiences and his relationships with God and others. Denver's spiritual process began with his new experiences. After reflecting upon them, he knew himself better. Knowing self is knowing one's spirit and knowing God's Spirit, who is revealed in the experiences of life. Thus, both nature and people nourished Denver's spirituality, which like biblical spirituality, results from a biblical author's experiences, his reflection upon them, and his simultaneous knowledge of himself and of the LORD. In this book the parallel Denver and biblical spirituality has been presented in an abecedarian format of sixty-seven themes of spirituality. Among those sixty-seven themes, are Denver's major entries of alone, dreams, God, heart, home, love, mountains, night, rain(bow), road, spirit, sun(down, set, shine, -ny), time, and wind. Out of all entries, Denver employs the sun—in all its forms of sundown, sunset, sunshine, and sunny—the most in presenting his natural spirituality. When it comes to presenting his relationship spirituality, the entry on love takes first place as the most used.

This book has guided the reader through repeated John Denver spirituality themes and paralleled them with similar biblical themes. A lengthy explanation of biblical spirituality is found in the introduction, which is followed by an application of Denver's spirituality so the reader can get the most out of both Denver's lyrics and biblical stories. Denver recognized the holiness of everything and everyone, as expressed in lyrics about nature and people, who nourished his spirituality.

Through the process of reflection on Denver's spirituality and his lifetime journey of living, growing, and becoming paralleled with biblical spirituality, the reader has not only reached a point of understanding both better, but he or she has also nourished and grown deeper in his or her spirituality. The fact that Denver's songs (lyrics and music) are still popular thirty years after his death indicates that his spirituality continues to nourish many, because it some way it echoes others' spirituality and simultaneously biblical spirituality.

BIBLIOGRAPHY

Holy Bible: New International Version. Grand Rapids, MI: Zondervan, 2023.

In the Garden. Unity Village, MO, 2025.

New American Standard Bible. La Habra, CA: Lockman Foundation, 2021.

O'Day, Gail R., David Peterson, eds. *The Access Bible: New Revised Standard Version with the Apocryphal/Deuterocanonical Books.* New York: Oxford University Press, 1999.

Okun, Milton, ed. *John Denver Anthology.* Chester, NY: Cherry Lane Music, 1982.

"The Order of Mass." In *The Roman Missal* (Study Edition), 511–673. Collegeville, MN: Liturgical, 2012.

Peterson, Eugene H., William Griffin, trans. *The Message: Catholic/Ecumenical Edition, The Bible in Contemporary Language.* Chicago, IL: ACTA, 2013.

DISCOGRAPHY

With the Mitchell Trio:
That's the Way It's Gonna Be (1965)
Violets of Dawn (1965)
Alive (1967)
Beginnings: John Denver with the Mitchell Trio (1974)

John Denver Sings (1966)
Rhymes and Reasons (1969)
Take Me to Tomorrow (1970)
Whose Garden Was This (1970)
Poems, Prayers and Promises (1971)
Aerie (1971)
Rocky Mountain High (1972)
Farewell Andromeda (1973)
John Denver's Greatest Hits (Volume I) (1973)
Back Home Again (1974)
Windsong (1975)
An Evening with John Denver (1975)
Rocky Mountain Christmas (1975)
Spirit (1976)
Live in London (1976)
I Want to Live (1977)
John Denver's Greatest Hits: Volume 2 (1977)
Live at the Sydney Opera House (1978)
J.D. (John Denver) (1979)
John Denver and the Muppets: A Christmas Together (1979)

Autograph (1980)

Some Days Are Diamonds (1981)

Perhaps Love (1981)

Seasons of the Heart (1982)

Rocky Mountain Holiday (1983)

It's About Time (1983)

John Denver's Greatest Hits: Volume 3 (1984)

Dreamland Express (1985)

One World (1986)

Higher Ground (1988)

Earth Songs (1990)

Stonehaven Sunrise: The Flower that Shattered the Stone (1990)

Christmas, Like a Lullaby (1990)

Different Directions (1991)

Take Me Home, Country Roads, and Other Hits (1991)

Favorites (1992)

A Portrait (1994)

The Very Best of John Denver (1994)

The Wildlife Concert (1995)

The John Denver Collection (1995)

The Rocky Mountain Collection (1996)

Reflections: Songs of Love & Life (1996)

Love Again (1996)

Country Roads Collection (1997)

All Aboard! (1997)

A Celebration of Life (1943–1997) (1997)

The Best of John Denver Live (1997)

The Best of John Denver (1998)

Greatest Country Hits (1998)

Forever, John (1998)

Live at the Sydney Opera House (1999)

Legendary John Denver (1999)

John Denver Christmas (1999)

Sing Australia (2001)

The Very Best of John Denver (2001)

Christmas in Concert (2001)

The Harbor Lights Concert (2002)

Songs for America (2002)

The Essential John Denver (2004)

Definitive All-Time Greatest Hits (2004)

A Song's Best Friend: The Very Best of John Denver (2004)

16 Biggest Hits (2006)
Live in the U.S.S.R. (2007)
The Essential John Denver (2007)
Playlist: The Very Best of John Denver (2008)
Live at Cedar Rapids (2010)
The Ultimate Collection (2011)
The Classic Christmas Album (2012)
All of My Memories: The John Denver Collection (2014)
The Windstar Greatest Hits (2017)
Gold (2019)
The Last Recordings (2023)

Recent Books by Mark G. Boyer
Published by Wipf & Stock

Nature Spirituality: Praying with Wind, Water, Earth, Fire

A Spirituality of Ageing

Weekday Saints: Reflections on Their Scriptures

Human Wholeness: A Spirituality of Relationship

A Simple Systematic Mariology

Praying Your Way through Luke's Gospel and the Acts of the Apostles

An Abecedarian of Animal Spirit Guides: Spiritual Growth through Reflections on Creatures

Overcome with Paschal Joy: Chanting through Lent and Easter—Daily Reflections with Familiar Hymns

Taking Leave of Your Home: Moving in the Peace of Christ

An Abecedarian of Sacred Trees: Spiritual Growth through Reflections on Woody Plants

Divine Presence: Elements of Biblical Theophanies

Fruit of the Vine: A Biblical Spirituality of Wine

Names for Jesus: Reflections for Advent and Christmas

Talk to God and Listen to the Casual Reply: Experiencing the Spirituality of John Denver

Christ Our Passover Has Been Sacrificed: A Guide through Paschal Mystery Spirituality—Mystical Theology in The Roman Missal

Rosary Primer: The Prayers, The Mysteries, and the New Testament

From Contemplation to Action: The Spiritual Process of Divine Discernment Using Elijah and Elisha as Models

Love Addict

All Things Mary: Honoring the Mother of God—An Anthology of Marian Reflections

Shhh! The Sound of Sheer Silence: A Biblical Spirituality that Transforms

What is Born of the Spirit is Spirit: A Biblical Spirituality of Spirit

Very Short Reflections—for Advent and Christmas, Lent and Easter, Ordinary Time, and Saints—through the Liturgical Year

Living Parables: Today's Versions

My Life of Ministry, Writing, Teaching, and Traveling: The Autobiography of an Old Mines Missionary

300 Years of the French in Old Mines: A Narrative History of the Oldest Village in Missouri

Journey into God: Spiritual Reflections for Travelers

Monthly Entries for the Spiritual but not Religious through the Year: Texts, Reflections, Journal/Meditations, and Prayers for the Spiritual but not Religious

The Shelbydog Chronicles by Shelby Cole as Recorded by Mark G. Boyer: A Novel

Four Catholic Pioneers in Missouri: Lamarque, Kenrick, Fox, and Hogan: Irish Missionaries and Their Supporter

Smothered with Inexhaustible Mercy: An Anthology of Poems

Spirituality for the Solitary: A Handbook for Those Who Live Alone

Seasons of Biblical Spirituality: Spring, Summer, Autumn, Winter

Biblical Names for God: An Abecedarian Anthology of Spiritual Reflections for Anytime

More Shelbydog Chronicles: Reflections on a Dog's Life by Her Friend, Knowing Your Pet

His Mercy Endures Forever: Biblical Reflections on Divine Mercy for Anytime

The Roman Catholic Lectionary and the Bible: Analysis, Conclusions, Suggested Alternatives

The Spirit of the Lord God: Biblical Names and Images for the Holy Spirit; An Abecedarian Anthology of Spiritual Reflections for Anytime

A Biblical Morning & Evening Prayer Manual: A Modern Book of Hours, Ways to Begin and End the Day

The Folks in the Woods: A Memoir of Brown Hollow, Missouri, 1874–1991

The Liturgical Environment: What the Documents Say about Roman Catholic Churches, Fourth Edition, Updated and Revised

Eavesdropping on Paul: Reading Others' Biblical Mail

Biblical Creation Stories: Plural Ways to Nourish Spirituality

www.ingramcontent.com/pod-product-compliance
Lightning Source LLC
Chambersburg PA
CBHW060355090426
42734CB00011B/2145